Footloose
Cornish Folklore

Margaret Caine & Alan Gorton

A Comfy Jack Book

First published in 2005 by Cotswold Quality (Leisure) Ltd.
4, Gables Court, Blackwell, Warwickshire CV36 4PE

ISBN   0 9541036 4 5

Cover design and artwork by NPD Design Consultants, Shipston-on-Stour   CV36 4AH
Printed and bound by R Booth Ltd
Antron Hill, Mabe, Penryn, Cornwall TR10 9HH

*C*ontents

Introduction

This book has wide appeal. It is essential reading for anyone interested in folklore, in walking, and in combining the two. By vividly bringing to life the legendary heroes, alluring mermaids, terrifying giants, mischievous piskeys and infamous wreckers together with exhilarating walks specially designed to give you the excitement of seeking out their locations, stepping over the very ground they trod, it doubles the pleasure. You will visit remarkable places which might be atmospheric, peaceful, brooding or offer a magnificently high, windy viewpoint, dramatic cliffs, crescent-shaped sandy beaches, sheltered creeks of lazy rivers and stark moors ancient and unspoiled. This is the essence of where you will walk. But there is more. The addition of imaginative stories adds a new dimension - a journey through both a real and a mythical landscape.

Not for nothing is Cornwall known as the 'Land of Legend'. Its folklore reaches to the mists of time with such a rich diversity, such a distinctive heritage, that scarcely a hamlet is without its own story. In this fascinating patchwork people live on the edge of two worlds, the material and the mysterious, where fact and fiction overlap - so here are real people, historical figures whose lives have been embroidered with help from the supernatural, sunken cities, village wenches turned into stone, all within a realm of fairies, spriggans and knockers, those curious creatures of the netherworld - reminders of a past so culturally different, more physically demanding and dangerous than our own times. This book illuminates this Cornish past and will enhance your interest in the county.

Here though is more than just a collection of the great and lesser known Cornish myths and legends. Necessarily we have been selective in choosing from the hundreds still surviving those which have caught our imagination or the versions we like best. Where there is a historical basis, we have consulted contemporary records. At the same time we have aimed to show how fine the county is on foot. To enable you to identify locations, map references are given using OS Landranger series. The maps accompanying each walk are intended for guidance only, and are not to scale. We would ask you, though, to park carefully and considerately in small villages and lanes and at all times to follow the Countryside Code.

Using this book, your journey will be one of exploration of the quality that makes Cornwall a place apart. We hope it will inspire you to follow in our footsteps and experience the thrill of discovery for yourselves. It has not been possible to do justice to the whole county in one volume, so this one has a companion, *Walking in Cornish Folklore*, which covers the rest of the county.

Now we shall a tale unfold ...

Margaret Caine and Alan Gorton

ST AGNES

WAS BEANSTALK JACK A SERIAL KILLER?

The landscape here is eerily beautiful. It was very different three hundred years ago when tin was the powerhouse of Cornwall's economy and its miners claimed "*Sten Sen Agnes an Gwella sten yu Kernow*", 'St Agnes tin is the best tin in Cornwall'. Now the only sound comes from the haunting screech of seagulls but then the oak wooded, heather topped valleys were a clattering valhalla of stamps and crushing wheels producing their hard-won precious metals, tin, copper, iron, lead and silver, throbbing with the racket. Thousands of brave, determined, hardy miners made their home along this stretch of coast. After their shift they gathered in taverns to entertain each other with stories of boy-eating giants.

The miners' tales had been doing the rounds for centuries, evolving and changing in this heartland of the tin industry, yet it was not until 1708 that Jack-the-giant-slayer's story was first published. *Jack and the Gyants* tells of a Cornish farmer's son who meets and kills numerous monsters. He then makes off with their gold and enriches his struggling parents. No mention of a beanstalk in these early tales - that was added by the Victorians. The early Jack tales were gory, brutal, lacking in romance, and his murder weapon was a tin miner's pick. Indeed, Jack sounds more like a serial killer than an innocent little boy. There is more, for in these old tales Jack-the-giant-slayer went on to become a servant of King Arthur at Tintagel, fifty miles up the coast. Since then it has become confused with Jack and the Beanstalk, in which Jack exchanges his mother's cow for a handful of beans which miraculously produce stalks reaching to the sky. Jack climbs up and steals from the ogre's castle a bag of gold and a hen which lays golden eggs, thus relieving their poverty.

Come here in the evening twilight, when the wind is howling off the sea, walk among the oak copses dotted with derelict stacks and defunct engine houses, remnants which bear stark testament to those miners and their wives, and you'll soon find the ghosts of Jack's forebears. What's that ogre-shaped shadow? Is that young lad carrying a blood-drenched pick? In this corner of Cornwall you'll find a very different Jack from the one on the panto stage.

... BUT NOT OF GIANT BOLSTER ...

Are you trying to tell us that giants didn't exist? Cornwall is a land of giants. They stride through the landscape eating children, burying treasure or hurling massive rock quoits. What other explanation could there be for the stone structures which dominate moorland hilltops? Possibly the stories started in a simple way, a natural explanation to incursions by taller, economically dominant Anglo-Saxons. From this could have sprung tales not only of Jack-the-giant-slayer but also of the picturesquely named Giant Bolster. However, a genuine Cornish giant was discovered in 1861 when a group of tin miners unearthed a coffin at Tregony: the box was over eleven feet long and the corpse inside had a tooth measuring two-and-a-half inches. Elsewhere, skeletons of other unusually tall men have been unearthed though as yet none large enough to have stood with one foot on St Agnes Beacon, an impressive landmark 629 feet (161.5m) above sea level, and the other on Carn Brea six miles away: but Bolster could.

Legend has it that Giant Bolster and the giant who lived on Carn Brea had a long-standing feud, hurling rocks at each other across the intervening miles. Bolster was the more aggressive and completely denuded his Beacon of granite, throwing most of the huge missiles which now lie around Cran Brea. In readiness for these rock fights, Bolster's opponent heaped rocks at intervals along the Carn's summit, to provide ammunition, and the piles, ample evidence of his presence, can still be seen at the Castle, the Monument, Tortoise Rock and Tregarjorran Carn, where he is said to be buried. We even know what he looked like. When viewed from the west, the Giant's Head or Face Rock bears a strong resemblance to his face looking towards St Agnes Beacon. Another part of his body, the Giant's Hand, is broken in two, but ridges and depressions certainly resemble his huge hand.

One wonders how this stone-throwing legend came about. Could it possibly embody an actual feud between two chieftains who led tribes on these hills in ancient times?

'Bolster' is an unusual name. It appears to derive from the Cornish *both-lester*, meaning 'an upturned boat', and certainly the ancient two-mile earthwork Bolster Bank below St Agnes Beacon, which was supposedly raised by the giant, resembles one near Bolster Farm. If you want further proof of his enormous size, a stone in the valley running inland from Chapel Porth contains the impression of the giant's fingers. On that occasion Bolster, feeling thirsty after one of his mighty strides, stopped to drink out of the well, resting his hand on this stone: the outline has been here ever since.

It is not often that we hear of giant's wives but Bolster's endured a life of continuous, futile labour. On top of St Agnes Beacon are piles of relatively small stones. Most of the farms around here have been claimed from the moorland and even after centuries still have stones mixed with the soil: in just one, at the foot of the hill next to the village, are they remarkably absent. This is because whenever Bolster became angry with his wife he bullied her into collecting these stones and carrying them to the top of the hill.

Clearly Giant Bolster was a complex character. Like most of his colleagues, though physically enormous, he was an emotionally simple soul. He fell in love with a local girl, St Agnes, but couldn't see that they were hopelessly mismatched and any relationship was doomed. He was immense, shambling, ugly and uncouth; she was tiny, devout, virtuous, sworn to chastity. Nonetheless, he gave her no rest. Wherever she went he followed, proclaiming his love and filling the air with his sighs, asking only to be with her and always in the hope that one day she might feel able to return his affections. Not surprisingly, St Agnes grew tired of his advances until, finding the situation intolerable, she devised a most unsaintly scheme to bring it to an end. Pretending to take him seriously, she asked him to prove his love by filling a hole in the cliff above Chapel Porth with his blood: what the cunning saint knew but the simple giant did not was that the hole was bottomless and opened directly into the sea below.

Bolster was overjoyed to accept the condition. This was going to be quick and easy. He would barely miss the small amount of blood it would take to fill the hole. He had plenty to spare. He lay down, stretched out his huge arm and plunged a knife into a vein, watching the blood gush out and into the hole. He wouldn't have to wait long until it filled up. At first he was just surprised it was taking more blood than he had anticipated, but when hour after hour it poured from his vein he became too faint to realise what was happening - and still his blood flowed on. He died, murmuring St Agnes's name. The saint had got rid of her nuisance. The giantess was released from her tyranny. To this day the cliff at Chapel Porth bears a red stain, marking the route of Bolster's blood as it ran down to the sea.

... DORCAS' GHOST WAS NOT ALWAYS MISCHIEVOUS

While giants lived above ground and were readily visible to us mortals, ghosts, apparitions and spirits of every shape and size haunted the shafts and levels of the mines, many of them bringing disaster to the workers. One is here.

An old lady called Dorcas lived in a cottage near Polbeen Mine at the foot of St Agnes Beacon. Tired, care-worn, weary of her lonely life, one night she had had enough and threw herself down into the deep shaft. Her broken body was recovered and though she was buried with as much ceremony as suicide would allow, her spirit lived on in the mine - and began to play tricks on the miners. Her voice could often be heard calling the tinners by name, luring them away from their work - and as they were on piecework this was important - or tearing their shirts from their backs. On one occasion however Dorcas' ghost forgot her mischief and saved a miner from certain death. Two tinners were at work in Darkey's Shaft when between the blows of their hammer one of them heard his name being called. Both stopped and listened: nothing happened. They continued but after another blow on the iron rod the name was called again, louder and more insistently. The man dropped his heavy tools and set off to find who-ever it was who wanted him. He had walked only a few yards when a massive rock-fall of many tons crashed down from the roof onto the very spot where he had been standing. No miner had been calling his name. Until his death he swore that Dorcas had saved his life.

WALK DIRECTIONS

Distance 5½ miles (7.4km)   Time   3 hours
Map   OS Landranger 203 722516 Terrain Some modest slopes along coastal paths
                                     and an inland climb to 600 feet (192m)
Car Parking   Park in the official District Council car park.

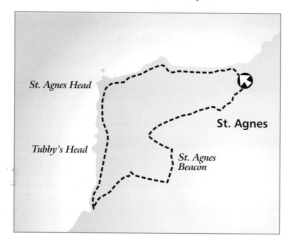

>>   From the car park go down the adjacent lane towards the sea, turning off right to
     follow the path down the left side of the lookout post to join the Coast Path at St
     Agnes Head. Few Cornish headlands are more spectacular.
     *St Agnes herself had an eventful life. Unlike most of Cornwall's saints she was
     thought to have been a Roman of high social standing who rejected the hand of a
     non-Christian suitor. Subsequently, she was condemned to be burned alive but the
     flames formed a circle around the stake and left her untouched. Later she was
     beheaded - still only at the tender age of thirteen.*

>>   Turn left on the Coast Path and follow this for about 2½ miles (3.5km), passing
     Tubby's Head, and on to Chapel Porth.
     *You will pass Towanroath Engine House built in 1872 perched on a dangerous
     ledge above the sea. The great steam pump worked a piston that went down the
     shaft you can see covered with an iron grill, to suck the water out of Wheal Coates
     mine. This, with its three-storeyed stamp and whim houses, reached peak
     production in the 1870s but it was never very profitable, producing just over a
     thousand tons of ore, mainly tin, from 1815 until it closed in 1889.*

>>   At Chapel Porth is the hole which St Agnes persuaded Giant Bolster to fill with
     his blood - look at the red stain it made down the cliff face all the way to the sea.
     *Chapel Porth gets its name from a holy well and chapel built here in the Dark
     Ages. You can find the remains of the chapel by taking the signed path going
     inland - within a few yards its outline appears to the right of the path. Nothing
     remains of the well, which in pagan times was supposed to have oracular and
     therapeutic properties. During the eighteenth century the water from the well
     began to drain into the workings of Charlotte United, East Charlotte and Wheal
     Freedom mines, so in 1780 both it and the chapel were demolished.*

Just further inland is the Giant's Footprint imprinted into the rock: some say it is a huge natural feature, but are you sure it is not where Bolster actually stood?

The sea always appears an innocent, inviting pale turquoise here but is not to be trusted. The Porth served as a landing point for the mines but was abandoned because of the sea's unpredictability and fickleness.

\>\>   Walk up the road to the higher footbridge. From here take the path going inland, which emerges in a car park. Turn left up the road (Beacon Drive) until you reach the first lane on your right. Go through Beacon Farm, keeping to the public right of way following the lane around the farmyard.

Clay was excavated from here to make waterproof foundations for piers, such as the ones in Penzance harbour. The famous potter Bernard Leach used it, too.

Continue to the right of the cottages, up a track across a field to the stone stile, with the hedge on your left, and across heathland until you reach National Trust land at the base of the Beacon.

As with other beacons, fires have always been lit here on special occasions, to warn or to celebrate. It is possible that centuries ago this included the annual Celtic pagan fire festival of Beltane in May.

\>\>   Continue along the base of the hill until you reach the wide path on your left. Take this and climb the shoulder of the hill to the triangulation point at the top.

The Beacon has interesting geological strata, made up of sedimentary killas above the granite. Around the hill near the top is a layer of grey clay used by early miners to attach candles to their felt hats and below this is a stratum of sand and pebbles which they claimed was the high-water mark of Noah's Flood - but more likely indicates that 50 million years ago the sea was at this level or earth movements have lifted the rock. The sand has been quarried for hundreds of years, for glass-making or moulds in smelting works.

From here Giant Bolster could stand on one foot while placing the other on Carn Brea almost due south, which you can identify from the tall Basset (de Dunstanville) monument crowning its top.

It was never easy for mine-owners to locate rich lodes of ore, but they could be indicated by the presence at ground level of small, dancing lights called 'Jack o' Lantern's'. In 1850 the fortunes of North Basset mine, Camborne, were turned round by these. An old woman called Grace who lived nearby claimed to have seen the Jack o' Lanterns and, knowing the mine was in financial difficulty, pointed out the spot and advised the shareholders, or 'adventurers', to sink a shaft there. They ignored her, but their situation deteriorated until in desperation they agreed to follow her advice. There they found one of the richest deposits of copper and other minerals ever discovered. In her honour it was named 'Grace's Shaft', and as a mark of their gratitude the old woman was granted five shillings a month from its profits, together with a smart new gown every year.

If you look to the north you will see less than half a mile away the ruins of the mine into which poor old Dorcas threw herself.

The views from here are breathtaking. You can see a total of thirty church towers, Trencrom Hill, the St Austell china-clay mining area and Trevose Head.

The cairns near to the main path are ancient Bronze Age burial mounds - it's no wonder prehistoric man chose this spot to bury his dead.

\>\>   From the top of the Beacon two paths lead off along the ridge towards the sea. Continue along the plateau until a wide path leads down to your left. Follow this to where you have parked your car.

PORTREATH

GIANT WRATH ...

If you prefer not to meet up with Giant Bolster, how about a confrontation with Giant Wrath? Here on the coast at this narrowest part of Cornwall he certainly lived up to his name as the dread of all sea-farers.

In the cliffs near Portreath is a large fissure which we now call 'Ralph's Cupboard'. At one time it was different, a fully-formed cavern. From here Wrath lay in wait for any passing fishing boats, going to or from St Ives. He was particularly interested in those unfortunate sailors who drifted into this cavern but even if boats passed within a mile he would wade out, club the sailors with his huge, thick fingers, and drag them back to his cavern. Here he examined the sailors more closely. Thin ones he threw back into the sea but plump young men he kept in his larder, the 'Cupboard': for the staple diet of this ferocious monster was well-fed sailors. Even ships sailing in deeper water were not safe. Many were sunk when he flung rocks at them from the clifftop, rocks which you can still see at low tide forming the dangerous reef stretching out from Godrevy Head.

St Ives fishermen believed that nothing came out of the 'Cupboard' which had the misfortune to be drawn in by the unpredictable seas around this coast, so are you surprised that it remained a place best avoided or paid close attention to what they were doing when they got near? Would they have been wiser to keep to their own diet, boring and repetitive as it undoubtedly was, of oily mackerel, potatoes and conger eel? Until one day that is when during a terrific storm a flock of sheep grazing on the slopes at Gwithian nearby were blown into the sea and hauled up along with the catch of pilchards. The town dined well that night according to Fortescue Hitchin in 1800, and thus started the annual feast of mutton:

> Now those who had to feed on fish
> Ten minutes took to enjoy that dish,
> An hour now to dinner linger
> To pick the bones and lick the finger.

'Ralph's Cupboard' is no longer a cavern. The roof collapsed when Giant Wrath died, leaving us with the open chasm through which the sea flows at high tide.

... AT LEAST ONE SMUGGLER CHEATED JUSTICE

Vigilant as he was, Giant Wrath didn't manage to catch every sailor around here.

Hell's Mouth lies to the east of Navax Point, sheltered from the wild Atlantic by razor-sharp rocks. At the base of the sheer 350-foot-high cliffs is a network of tunnels and caves which for centuries were used by smugglers to hide their contraband. Two brothers were active members of a gang and acquired a reputation of being ruthless, nasty pieces of work, terrorising the local residents and causing as much mayhem as possible. But after many years of patient detective work the Excise men caught the gang, among them the younger of the brothers. All were hanged in public. As if in revenge the older brother increased his nefarious 'free-trading' activities. The authorities also increased their attempts to catch him and after several months he was cornered on the cliffs at Hell's Mouth. There was no escape.

In a tempestuous storm he stood in the darkness, the wind raging around him, the ferocious sea beneath. He faced the same fate as his brother. That was not his way. He gave one last defiant shout and jumped over the edge to certain death. The Excise men heard his blood-curdling scream as he plunged to the rocks below. They looked over the cliffs to see his crumpled, lifeless body being dragged out by the boiling waters. Ever since, in stormy weather, the cries and scream of the smuggler can be heard in the howling wind.

WALK DIRECTIONS

Distance	7½ miles (11km)	Time	3½ hours
Map	OS Landranger 203 657456	Terrain	Mainly level on Coast Path and public footpaths. There are two hard climbs from sea-level up to 200 feet (80m) at the beginning of the walk.
Car Parking	Park in the car park near the shore at Portreath just before you go over a bridge.		

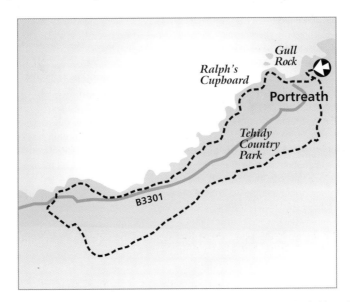

>> From the car park go on to the main road and turn right over the bridge, then almost immediately right again up Battery Hill. Walk along this road to the end, passing two garages and following a sign to the left of them to the Coast Path. Head up Western Hill to join the Coast Path. Ahead, out to sea, is Gull Rock.

>> Follow the Coast Path as it bends to the left with the sea and a beach on your right. Where it bends again to your right you will see in front of you the great, fierce gorge of Ralph's Cupboard.

This is where Giant Wrath stored his booty of well-fed sailors. You are standing on the spot he did as he watched out for St Ives fishermen before rushing down the beach and wading into the sea to snatch them from their boats, or throwing huge boulders to sink ships which were further out.

>> Follow the Coast Path for another 2½ miles (3.5km), passing Bassett's Cove, with Crane Islands offshore, to the car park on Reskajeage Downs on the cliff top. Continue along the path, passing above Deadman's Cove and Derrick Cove, before reaching Hell's Mouth where the road almost reaches the cliff.

>> Now you leave the Coast Path to go inland. Cross the road and walk through the gate to the left of and just behind the cafe. Turn right and pass through another gate, then continue along the side of the copse. Go through the next gate on your left and yet another on your right. Within a few yards you will see a stone building, where you turn left. Cross the stream and go into the field by the gate ahead, keeping to the hedge on your left, through another gate then across the next field which you leave at the gate onto a road. Turn left and walk about 300 yards (275m) before turning right over the low stile directly opposite the concrete farm road.

>> Follow the field edge to the next stile on your left, then continue ahead to go through a gate on the left. Walk straight downhill before joining the field boundary on your left. Go through the large gate, bear left past the farm buildings and continue down this track until you join the road. Cross this and in about 75 yards (70m) take the track on your right across some stepping stones. Walk along this track following the bottom of the valley near the river, then go over a wooden bridge onto the road.

>> Take the track which is directly across the road, going over the stile, down the left side of the fields and onto the lane where it turns left for about 250 yards (200m) to a track that shares the entrance with the house on the left. Follow this track, past the house and through Oak Wood for about 1 mile (1.6km).

>> When you come to a junction with other paths, turn left to the corner of the fields and then right onto a track until you reach a crossing with other tracks. Continue straight ahead, keeping the golf course on your right, to a small gate which you can see ahead. Go through and continue until you join a path which has a fence between the path and the golf course. After about 50 yards (47m) where the fence on your right bears away, follow the path which goes off left to the Tehidy Country Park car park.

>> Go across the car park, turn right on the road and then immediately left onto the track alongside the wood which forms part of the Country Park. Follow this to the farm, then turn left at the junction with a concrete farm road and take the first concrete farm road on your right down into the farmyard.

>> As the road enters the yard take the footpath near the fence which descends into the wood on your left. Follow this down and to the right and then take the path off to the left continuing through the valley to a lane, where you turn left.

>> At the next lane turn left again and at the bottom of the hill go under a small tunnel of the dismantled railway. Bear right over the bridge and then turn left to return to where you have parked your car, which you will reach shortly on your right.

ROSEWARNE

A GHOSTLY VISIT

Many generations of the De Rosewarne family had lived in their mansion before financial difficulties forced them to sell the estate. In what would now be regarded as a conflict of interest it was bought by Ezekiel Grosse, a lawyer who had been legal adviser to the family and who many felt had been less than honest with them. Scarcely had he moved in than one very dark night he saw in the park a ghost of a weary, care-worn, old man. Grosse paid little attention, until later when he was in his office examining a set of deeds and feeling irritated after losing an important case, the ghost appeared in the house. "*In the name of God, what wantest thou?*" asked Grosse. "*To show thee, Ezekiel Grosse, where the gold for which thou longest lies buried,*" came the reply.

Grosse certainly brightened up at the thought. The ghost beckoned and Grosse followed out of the room and into the park. Through the darkness it glided in front, giving off a light which guided him to a small valley in which was a heap of granite boulders. The ghost stared straight into the lawyer's eyes, and in low, measured, echoing tones: "*Ezekiel Grosse, thou longest for gold, as I did but I could not enjoy it. Heaps of treasure are buried beneath these stones; it is thine if thou diggest for it. Glitter with the wicked ones of the world; and when thou art the most joyous I will look in upon thy happiness.*" With this, it disappeared.

Ezekiel Grosse made a careful note of the spot. All night he considered what to do, until finally deciding to examine the heap in secret. A few nights later he moved the stones with an iron bar and dug into the ground. After only a few strokes his spade struck a bronze urn. He lifted the lid and saw it was full of old gold coins. He took as many as he could, and returned each night to get more until all the treasure was in Rosewarne House.

From now on Ezekiel Grosse led the life of a country gentleman. Neighbouring gentry discussed the additions and improvements to his mansion and grounds, local folk gossiped about the change in his personal appearance, former colleagues noted he had abandoned his legal practice. Everywhere he went he paraded his wealth ostentatiously. He surrounded himself with sycophants. The lawyer who had struggled hard to acquire wealth and did not always use honest means to get it was now able to preach the virtues of honesty.

Christmas Eve arrived. Rosewarne had attracted a large gathering of lords, ladies and gentlemen, dancing, drinking and dining. The night was going with a swing. Until every-one felt a chill. There, in the middle of the hall, was a strange old man, looking angrily, in silence, at Ezekiel Grosse - and he was transfixed with terror. In less than a minute the old man was gone. Grosse tried to laugh the incident off as part of the festivities, but one by one the guests made excuses and left. All was not right at Rosewarne.

Grosse continued to hold various social events but each time the old man took his place in the middle of the table, never speaking but affecting everyone with his presence. He just rose, stared at the host, laughed demoniacally and left as quietly as he had come. Not surprisingly people began to turn down Grosse's invitations, his friends no longer contacted him, his servants left, until the only one remaining was his clerk, John Call.

From now on the ghost appeared more and more frequently. Wherever Grosse went, the aged man was by his side. Grosse deteriorated physically and psychologically, becoming bowed, miserable and constantly in fear. Things got so bad he offered to give up all his wealth if only the haunting would stop. The ghost agreed - provided the transaction was carried out in a perfectly legal manner and in favour of John Call. Even then Grosse tried to find ways of retaining at least some part of his property, but John Call became the rightful owner of Rosewarne and all its adjoining lands. Only then did the spirit explain that it was one of the ancestors of the De Roswarnes, and was allowed to return to earth for the express purpose of inflicting a suitable punishment on the avaricious lawyer. Ezekiel Grosse lived for only a short time, in poverty and misery. He died, people said, of some form of violence for various marks were found on his body. Others said they saw the ghost of De Rosewarne rejoicing among a group of demons as they carried Grosse's soul over Carn Brea.

TRENCROM HILL

GIANTS ARE HERE ...

Now the Giant of Trecrobben spent a lot of time on the top of Trencrom Hill. It was one of his favourite places. Like all giants at that time (and there were many in Cornwall) he enjoyed throwing rocks and other huge objects to the others while having the most striking panoramic views in every direction. From here he could see St Michael's Mount, and played his throwing games with Giant Cormoran who lived there. It is one thing to read about these two tossing rocks to one another with the same ease as you might throw a pebble but then climb to the top of Trencrom Hill and see the huge, rough, granite boulders that Cormoran threw in this direction strewn all over the hillside - indeed the ground is positively littered with them lying just as if thrown from a distance - and you will just begin to wonder. Was the National Trust's enormous Bowl Rock, at the foot of Trencrom Hill, one of these? It was certainly thrown there by a giant.

In fact Trecrobben was the centre of a region full of giants. They even built a castle on the summit, its four remaining entrances indicating the Herculean strength by which they piled the huge rocks on top of each other - though some experts say it was built by Iron Age people. Here the giants lived, foraging into the countryside, dragging their captives along the serpentine road up the hill before sacrificing them on the great flat rocks inside their castle.

It was in Morvah where Jack-the-giant-killer slew one of them, a cruel one who was terrorising the neighbourhood. Jack had attended a wedding ceremony, but not being interested in the hurling and wrestling amused himself by throwing stones at the giant's house on the top of the hill. Out came the giant roaring like thunder, terrifying the wedding guests. Jack then tormented the giant by pulling faces at him and challenging him to a fight. Roaring even louder, the giant charged down the hill - and disappeared! He had fallen into an enormous hole and now lay at the bottom, groaning and shaking. Jack knew there was an adit level driven into the hill and had removed the roof so that when the giant clumbered over the ground it collapsed. Quickly, Jack and the others piled rocks onto the giant, crushing him to death - and his bones lie there to this day, underneath the large rock called the Giant's Grave.

It had been the habit of this particular giant to walk up to Bosprenis Croft on the first day of August each year and perform magic. This was the one day when he was harmless, so the villagers gathered to watch and drink his health. After the giant had been killed the gathering was kept up and thus started Morvah Feast.

... AND SPRIGGANS

Before he died the Giant of Trecrobben buried an enormous horde of gold and jewels deep in the heart of this hill. Perhaps that is why the spriggans came here in the first place, to guard it. Spriggans were a race of warrior fairies, grotesquely ugly, believed by some to be the ghosts of giants who could alter their size and even change their features at will. And they were troublesome to humans. Hordes of them, hissing maliciously, spitting, grinning malevolently, protected every granite cairn where treasure might be buried as well as the ancient barrows and prehistoric dolmens beneath which, it was thought, gold and jewels lay beside the remains of pagan peoples who walked these moorlands thousands of years ago. It was their appointed task. But as well as being guardians of ancient places, they were responsible for raising storms, destroying buildings and crops and, like the piskeys, for stealing children and leaving changelings of their own kind.

One young man heard of this giant's legacy. He learned as much as he could about it from the old people until he was confident he could identify its exact location. So one clear, moonlit night he climbed the hill to measure out the ground, then set to work with pick and shovel. Immediately the weather changed - something was wrong! The sky grew dark as heavy clouds hid the moon and blotted out the moor, leaving the treasure-hunter in total darkness. A cold, damp wind whined among the rocks. Frightful crashes of thunder were followed by startling flashes of lightning. Anxiety turned to fear but he continued to dig. That is until one brilliant flash lit up the moorland. To his horror he saw a swarm of spriggans, everywhere, coming out of the ground itself, even out of the boulders, at first tiny then growing in size until they were almost giants as they moved menacingly towards him. Badly shaken, shrieking loudly, he dropped his spade and bolted down the hillside as if his life depended on it - which it probably did! Reaching his house he rushed inside, barricaded the door with heavy furniture, got into bed, covered himself up and prayed.

Traumatised, in deep shock, it took him a long time to recover. He was soon struggling financially but nothing could persuade him to make another attempt to find the Giant's gold! The spriggans were successful yet again in guarding the treasure of Trencrom Hill.

Then there was the old miner's widow who lived at Chyangweal, near the open mine-workings on Worvas Hill, not far from Trencrom Hill. These spriggans were notorious thieves and for some reason best known to themselves used her cottage to share out their spoils while she, supposedly, slept. Perhaps they thought they could trust her. After each visit, to show their appreciation for her help they always left her a few small coins by her bed, so she could buy one or two of life's little luxuries. But the old woman wanted more. She planned to steal it all.

One night she lay in bed as the spriggans gathered together an unusually large amount of gold and jewellery. It got better: the spriggans seemed to be arguing amongst themselves about how to divide it up. Now was the time. She knew no spriggan could harm you if you turn your coat inside out, so huddling under her bedclothes she turned her night-dress inside out, then jumped out and grabbed a gold cup. Alarmed, the spriggans scampered away leaving all their treasure - most of them, that is. As one dashed from the cottage he passed his hand over the old woman's night-dress. Now, though, she was rich beyond her wildest dreams. She left Chyangweal and bought a grand house in St Ives, where she lived the life of a lady. But there was one problem. Whenever she put on her night-dress she was tortured beyond endurance. None of the doctors could help, creams and salves didn't cure it. But those who had experience of these things knew the spriggans had got their own back - again!

ST IVES

A PHANTOM SHIP ...

One night many years ago, a gig's crew was called out to a ship in need of help to the west of St Ives Head. She was a schooner-rigged vessel with a light over her bows by which they could clearly see the hull: she was also a foreign trader, so here was a rich reward!

The men pulled hard on the oars and the helmsman steered with exceptional skill, so it wasn't long before he was calling out that they were almost ready to board the ship. The seaman rowing the bow oar prepared to spring aboard. The gig came closer and the rowers could see the ship's crew. As the bow-oar man leant across to get hold of the bulwarks his hand found nothing solid to hold onto and he lost his balance. Fortunately he was caught by one of his mates and dragged back into the gig instead of into the water. Then ship and lights disappeared.

The next morning the *Neptune* of London, commanded by Captain Richard Grant, was found wrecked at Gwithian, and all on board had perished. The captain's body and that of his son were picked up a few days later. Both were buried in Gwithian churchyard.

... A DROWNED SAILOR ...

On another occasion one of the St Ives' pilots went down to the harbour to see if he could find work. In the bay, waiting for the tide to bring her into Hayle harbour, was the merchant ship *Sally*. As the pilot was walking near the White Hart he noticed a man leaning against a post and as sailors do greeted him, and asked the time. He got no answer, so he repeated his question. Still no reply. Now annoyed he went nearer to give the man a piece of his mind - and saw his eyes were glaring, his mouth sagging open, there was seaweed and bits of wood in his beard, his skin looked as if it had been in water for some time.

Unsettled, the pilot walked away but the stranger followed, water squelching in his boots at every step. This was spooky. The pilot quickened his pace and, looking over his shoulder to see if he was still being followed, saw the stranger standing motionless. At this the pilot ran as fast as he could - but when he arrived at his crew's house there was the man, in the doorway, grinning. Now the pilot was really frightened. He called out and a man came to the door, saying he was the captain and gave the pilot the task of bringing the *Sally* into harbour.

The sequence of events had taken their toll though, and the pilot was feeling so unwell as he set off to walk home to St Ives he had to be carried by a carter. Three days later all his hair fell out and when it eventually re-grew it was as white as snow. For the next six months he was very ill but when he recovered he learned that on that very Saturday afternoon in the Spring of 1862 when these events were taking place the *Sally* had been wrecked off St Ives.

... AND A VICTIM OF THE SEA

A couple of centuries ago a series of violent storms shook the coast around St Ives, driving a number of ships onto the rocks. One evening as the light was fading a large ship appeared out of the dusk, sailing perilously close to the shore. Those watching knew there was little hope as the sailors aboard fought desperately to save her. The cruel seas tore the ship from her anchors while the ferocious wind shredded her sails. She struck a rock and her masts broke as wave after wave swept over her, dragging the sailors to their deaths.

The St Ives lifeboat was launched and its brave crew managed to bring their boat sufficiently close for ropes to be thrown across the boiling sea. They watched as a group of sailors appeared on the deck of the ship with a lady holding a child in her arms. Clearly they were pleading with her to hand the child to one of the sailors while she got herself ashore. Equally clearly, she was refusing. The ship was breaking up fast as the lady and her child were lowered into the raging torment. The crew on the lifeboat dragged them through the towering waves but as she lost consciousness the child slipped from her arms.

Before dawn the doomed ship had disintegrated and its timbers littered the shore. The lady recovered consciousness only to be told she had lost her child. Later that morning she died of grief. As she was being buried in the old churchyard along with other victims, those who had gathered for the funeral service saw a lady pass over the boundary wall and onto the beach towards the Island. There she spent hours amongst the rocks, searching for her little baby. Unable to find it she returned to her grave, sighing deeply and crying silently. On stormy nights the lady can still be seen, carrying a lantern to help her searching. No wonder local fishermen and their wives look on her appearance as an omen of impending disaster.

TOWEDNACK

KNOCKERS ARE HERE

Ever since St Piran discovered tin, it has been regarded as a treasure bringing wealth to a few and hard, dangerous work in appalling conditions for the many. It is easy to see why the tinners became superstitious and believed so determinedly in the existence of elfin creatures who lived exclusively in the mines and to whom they attributed the strange noises frequently heard underground. These were the mysterious knockers. Few miners have actually seen them but all who have describe small, withered, dried-up creatures with large ugly heads, large hooked noses, mouths slit from ear to ear, and emaciated, spindly, ungainly arms and legs - and always pulling the most dreadful faces. Knockers haunted the lower levels of the mines, where they were expert at locating the richest veins of ore, and indeed occasionally showed miners where these were - but they were also capricious if annoyed and extremely spiteful if not shown the respect they thought they were due. No wonder the tinners agreed the knockers needed careful handling and were wary of them: it was a brave - or foolish - man who did not leave a morsel from his pasty to placate them.

Some say they were the spirits of old miners but others that they had descended from a long-lost tribe that inhabited Cornwall before the Celts, their spirits not good enough for Heaven, too good for Hell, and thus condemned to haunt the underground where they began to decrease in height until ultimately they would disappear altogether. Knockers never worked on Christmas Day, Easter Day and All Saints' Day so tinners too preferred not to work on these festivals - though there have been reports of the creatures celebrating midnight mass in the deeper levels, singing carols in sweet, clear voices, accompanied by music from a mighty organ rumbling under the rock.

Despite all this, one Towednack miner, a man named Barker, was highly sceptical, claiming the knockers were mere superstitious figments of the imagination. He argued so much with his colleagues about their existence that one day one of the miners suggested he had nothing to lose by visiting a mine nearby where knockers had been heard frequently and by merely lying in the sunshine at the mouth of the shaft could watch for them. This he did. It wasn't long before he could hear the little creatures below whispering and chattering about how at the end of their eight-hour shifts they hid their tools until the next day. Barker had, for him, a brilliant idea: if he could discover this hiding place he could steal the tools and keep them for himself. So he listened more and more intently to the knockers' conversations - unaware that they knew he was there, that being spied on was one of their pet hates, and that his attitude towards them was inflammatory.

At last his luck had changed. Barker overheard one knocker say that after it had finished work it would leave its tools at a bend in the stream, another that it would leave them in a cleft of rocks, another under a bramble bush, another under ferns, and a last, very specific this time, declared loudly that it would leave them on Barker's knee - and at that instant a massive weight smashed down on his left knee. His yells and screams were met with malevolent laughter from the mineshaft. He was never scornful about the knockers again, but to his dying day walked with a limp. Sometimes he explained that this was caused by rheumatism brought on by dampness in the mine - but his fellow tinners knew differently.

WALK DIRECTIONS

Distance 8 miles (12.9km   Time   4 hours
Map   OS Landranger 203 517360   Terrain   Two steep hills, first up Worvas and later Trencrom Hills, otherwise an easy walk over fields, coastal paths and some roads.
Car Parking   Park in the National Trust car park at the bottom of Trencrom Hill.

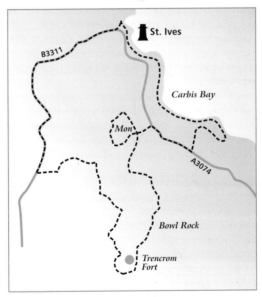

>>   Walk towards the road and turn left over the stile following the scalloped shell waymark of St Michael's Way. Keep to the track with Trencrom Hill on your left, going round the side of the hill through the bracken and gorse. When you reach a stile go over onto the road.

>>   Cross over and go through the gate opposite, bearing left and then immediately right, with the field hedge on your right. Walk down into the valley before bearing diagonally left and over the stile. Go down the steps, along the side of the house and continue straight ahead onto the track which leads down to the road.
Bowl Rock is 500 yards (470m) along the road to your right. This enormous round granite boulder was rolled here by a giant when playing bowls with a friend.

>> Cross the road and follow the St Michael's Waymark, going alongside the stream. When you reach a cottage bear left onto the track, now walking uphill. At the house at the top take the narrower path alongside it and continue between the high hedges to cross a stile. Keep to the fenced edge of the field and when you cross a stile turn right, this time walking alongside the hedge. Go over the stile on your right onto a tarmac lane.

>> Cross this lane and follow the St Michael's Waymark which is the first track on your left. Just before you reach farm buildings bear right into a field next to a large granite rock. Go across this field and over the stile ahead, and then along a short track to the stile into a caravan park. Walk diagonally left to join the public footpath at the right of the shower block. Follow the path ahead over a stile onto a lane.

>> Here, turn right and in a few yards take the first track on your left, passing the house on your right. Continue past Trewartha Farm and onto the narrow track which leads to the driveway of some cottages. As you pass the first of these on your left, turn left. Now you start to climb steeply. At the top, bear right between the cottages. When you reach the T-junction at the end of the lane, bear left and then almost immediately right through a kissing gate onto a public footpath. Continue ahead, ignoring all the other paths, until you go through a wooden kissing gate and onto a tarmac road.

>> Here, turn left, now ascending again until you reach the tarmac path signed 'Knill's Monument'. Turn left and walk up the hill to the monument. Standing with your back to the coat of arms, walk towards a gate and turn left onto a narrow track. When you reach a fork take the left hand path, following the St Michael's Waymark. This leads you down to surfaced Trencrom Lane, where you turn right.

>> Continue on this road to its junction with the A3074 St Ives-Lelant road. Cross over and continue down Portheptra Road opposite, signed 'Railway Station'. Pass the church and then turn right into Headland Road. When you reach Carrack Gladden cliff look to your right in the direction of Porth Kidney sands - this narrow overgrown track overlooking Carbis Bay is the home of a terrifying creature. *The very strange creature which haunts the cliff path is tall and its enormous head has no face - so it resembles a pumpkin. It moves in a peculiar jerky manner, swaying as it walks along the path before vanishing over the edge. Many people*

have been shocked by it but no-one has seen any trace it has left, either on the path or in its dive to the sea below.

>> From here follow the Coast Path waymark to your left, now climbing uphill until you reach the road where you turn right, passing the houses and walking in front of the Carbis Bay Hotel.

>> Still following the 'Coast Path' signs go past the Baulking House, a relic of the pilchard fishing industry, and straight over the cross-roads.

St Ives' fame came in the days of the pilchard fishing industry. Thirty million pilchards were caught in one hour in 1834. Another famous catch was recorded in 1868 when sixteen and a half million pilchards were caught in just one seine net. In this building the pilchards were piled into presses to extract the oil before being salted and packed into hogsheads to be exported to Mediterranean countries.

The track bends sharply right but you keep going ahead before bearing right down a narrow path, then some steps to Porthminster Beach

>> Walk through the gardens but when you arrive at the steps going uphill you keep straight on into The Warren, passing the artists' studios, towards the harbour. Go round the harbour following Wharf Road, turning left into Quay Street. At the end is Porthgwidden Beach.

In the nineteenth century a white horse and its rider were frequent visitors to Porthgwidden Beach, where the man would go for a swim while his mount waited on the sands. One evening the pair came as usual, but as the man was wading into the sea he was swept out by the rising tide. The white horse was later found wandering alone on the beach. It still returns to wait for its master - though it has also been seen with a figure on its back, presumably its unfortunate owner.

>> Walk out onto The Island where you may see the ghostly lady searching among the rocks for her drowned baby, and then follow the signs for B3311 to Halsetown, along which you walk for about 1¼ miles (2km) until you arrive at a junction signed 'Towednack' to your right.

St Tewennochus' church is a favourite with visitors but hides an eventful history. When the masons were building the tower the Devil came to inspect it every night. As it reached a certain height he knocked it down and stole the battlements and pinnacles. Next day day the work was renewed but each night the Devil undid it until in exasperation the builders gave up, swearing it was pointless to try to beat him, and left it at that height. That is why the tower still remains plain, squat and stark, and why the locals quote the proverb "There are no cuckolds in Towednack because there are no horns on the church tower."

>> Turn left, signed 'Vorvas'. Walk along this road and take the first road on your left, to Vorvas. Here ignore the first footpath sign but turn right onto the second signed footpath, going downhill to Nance, where you go over the stile onto the road. Turn left and walk along for a quarter of a mile (.4km), passing the junction before going over the stile onto the signed footpath on your right to Trencrom.

>> Turn left and walk past the houses on your left, until you reach a stile on your right displaying a National Trust acorn signed 'Trencrom Hill'. Take the footpath, climbing uphill to the granite-strewn summit and its stunning views.

You can explore the remains of the giants' castle (or Iron Age fort!) and the burial mounds which provoked the legend of the spriggans. But remember that they are watching you, too!

>> Keeping St Michael's Mount directly ahead, take the track which descends around a huge boulder balanced on a rock and leads to your car.

ZENNOR

FOR A MERMAID'S LOVE ...

In earlier times the hardy folk of Zennor lived in a world of their own tucked away in the shelter of Trewey Hill, far removed from other communities by land and unnoticed from the sea. The wild Atlantic governed their lives, its cruel winds howling across the bare and barren plateau and raging seas pounding relentlessly against the steep, unforgiving coastline.

One might expect the village to be remembered for swash-buckling exploits of skilful daring on the ocean, but this tale is about how a mermaid came to be immortalised on a bench-end in the parish church. It is an old carving, created five or six hundred years ago, and portrays, somewhat unflatteringly, a bare-breasted beauty with her comb in her left hand and her mirror in her right, waist-length hair and a scaly tail.

For some considerable time a fashionably-dressed young woman attended Sunday morning services at St Senara's church, where her exquisite singing enchanted generations of the congregation and her beauty captivated the men. There was a problem, though. Her identity remained a mystery. No-one knew her name or where she came from, only that people had seen her pass beyond Tregartha Hill, as after each service, immediately the vicar ended his final blessing, she walked out of the church and down the path towards Zennor Head - then vanished, to re-appear only the following Sunday to sit alongside the entrance door somewhat apart from the congregation. Moreover, unlike everyone else, as the years rolled by she showed no signs of ageing: time left her face unlined, her hair still golden. Not surprisingly she became the focus for local discussion, though she was so unapproachable people felt discouraged from talking to her directly.

Time passed by, and the pattern remained the same. Until one Sunday the mysterious lady saw young Matthew Trewella, the churchwarden's son and a chorister here. Matthew was a handsome fellow whose rich tenor voice, the finest for miles around, soared up into the church's barrel roof, and she returned again and again just to hear him sing. They must have exchanged glances week after week as clearly they were fascinated with each other.

Matthew waited for an opportunity and then spoke to her. Not long afterwards, after evensong, he was seen accompanying her away from the church down to the stream which runs in the direction of the cliffs. Neither attended church again. With a faint splash and a ripple on the surface they had both disappeared into the water of Pendour Cove. Not knowing this, everyone assumed the couple had eloped and left the district. Matthew's father though had an inkling. Seeking to flatter her and tempt her out of the sea, in the hope that at the same time she would give up his son, he ordered the sensuous mermaid to be carved on the bench-end. The woodcarver allowed himself full rein in his portrayal of feminine charm but neither the mermaid nor Matthew returned.

The story doesn't end there. It all remained a mystery until years later when a mermaid bobbed up from the sea and, flapping loudly on the water, politely asked the skipper of a ship anchored off Pendour Cove if he would move as his anchor was blocking the entrance to the cave where her husband Matthew and their mer-children were trapped inside. Of Matthew there was no sign, but the captain came from Zennor and recognised her as the strange lady who used to attend the church. Panic-stricken, he raised anchor faster than ever before and rushed for the safety of St Ives harbour. Soon the town was buzzing with news of this extraordinary event. For the folk of Zennor the mystery was solved - now they knew the true identity of the strange lady and what had happened to Matthew Trewella. He had gone with her to her watery habitat and been living on the sea-bed in Pendour Cove.

Don't take our word for it - go and look at the mermaid in Zennor church. Then, as you follow the walk, listen very carefully: on warm summer evenings when the sea is glassy calm and a gentle swell reflects the moon shimmering across the ripples, you can hear faintly drifting up from under the waves the pair of lovers singing melodiously together a quiet lullaby to their mer-children.

... TREVA - WHERE A WITCH DIED ...

Not only mermaids, but witches lived around Zennor. 'The Witches Rock' is where, tradition says, the Cornish covens met on Midsummer Eve. For ordinary humans who dared, touching it nine times at midnight was regarded as insurance against misfortune. We haven't tried it!

A long time ago, an old woman lived at Treva, a hamlet in Zennor. She was a witch, and her charms, spells and incantations scared most of her neighbours. Her husband though was not impressed. He didn't believe she had any supernatural powers at all, and made his opinions clear to anyone who would listen.

Until, that is, one day he came home ravenously hungry after a hard day's work, only to find that his meal had not been prepared. Worse still, there was no food at all in the house. He shouted and raged at his wife's incompetence but her only reply was, *"I can't get food out of the stones, can I?"* Her calmness made him even angrier, but he got no further explanation and certainly no dinner. Now, he began to wonder, was there just something in what people said about his wife and her black arts? He would test it for himself. As forthrightly as he could, he told her that he would be the death of her if she didn't prepare his dinner, but conversely if within half an hour she gave him a good cooked meal he would believe all she had said about her talents as a witch, and moreover submit to her every wish for the rest of his life. What a challenge!

Though St Ives, the nearest market town, was five miles away, the woman put on her outdoor clothes and set off along the road and down the hill as her husband watched from their cottage door. To his surprise, he saw his wife lie on the ground and vanish but from that very same spot appeared a full-grown hare which ran at full speed towards St Ives. Nonetheless, he kept his promise and waited. Surely enough, within the half hour into the cottage walked his wife with meat and potatoes all prepared for eating. All his scepticism was dispelled, and he lived in awe of his wife, the witch of Treva, until the day of her death.

In fact this came sooner than either had expected. She became ill. Her bedroom filled with evil spirits and at the moment of her death, though the sky outside was clear and blue, a black cloud settled over the cottage. As her coffin was being carried to the churchyard a hare started from the roadside and leaped over it. Startled, the bearers let the coffin fall and ran away as fast as they could. Another group of men lifted it and continued the procession. They hadn't gone far when a cat suddenly appeared and sat on it. Again the coffin was dropped. This time the vicar had difficulty persuading anyone to carry the old woman's body, and the men walked as quickly as they could with the vicar in front continuously repeating the Lord's Prayer. All went well until they arrived at the church stile and rested the coffin. The vicar paused to begin the burial service proper - and there stood the hare. As the vicar opened with "*I am the Resurrection and the Life*", the animal gave out a diabolical howl, changed into a black, malformed creature, and disappeared.

... THE GIANT OF CARN GALVER

Giants lived here too. Above Zennor granite outcrops stand starkly at the edge of the high moors, balanced one upon another in strange shapes. These were the playthings of the Giant of Carn Galver.

Unlike most Cornish giants, who were usually cruel and selfish, Holiburn was sensitive and playful, watching over the villages below from the rocking or logan stone he balanced on the most westerly hill of the range. Here he sat, protecting the folk of Zennor to the north and Morvah to the south from the quarrelsome, querulous, argumentative giants who lived on the Lelant hills and whose main interest in life was terrorising and being as troublesome as possible to their human neighbours. Near Holiburn's rocking seat are a pile of regular cuboid rocks with which he used to amuse himself, building one on top of the others then kicking them down again. Most of all though Holiburn liked playing 'bob button' with his friend, a young man from Chun whose quoit you can still see nearby. One day they had a thrilling contest and when it was time for his friend to return home the giant patted him good-naturedly on his head with the tips of his fingers, thanking him for coming and inviting him to another game the next day. To his horror the young man fell down at his feet: the giant's fingers had gone straight through his skull.

Realising the damage he had caused, Holiburn wailed out loud, rocking the young man in his arms. He could not comprehend why his friend's skull was so thin and delicate - unlike his own - nor the strength of his own fingers in what he thought was a gentle tap.

Giant Holiburn was overcome with guilt and grief. He was inconsolable, having no-one to play 'bob button' and hide-and-seek with. He pined away and shortly afterwards he died alone and forlorn. But the good people of Morvah did not forget him, for his memory is perpetuated annually in Morvah Fair.

... AND FRIENDS RE-UNITED

In the early years of the nineteenth century, after a long, hard but successful career at sea, James Bottrell came to Zennor, looking forward to a quiet, peaceful retirement in his twilight years. It was not to be.

Three loud knocks almost broke his bedroom window. As he struggled into wakefulness he was surprised to find a man standing by his bed. He was face to face with a former crew-member and best friend, John Jones - who had died some years previously! But this was not how James Bottrell remembered John Jones: now he was pale and distinctly care-worn. Before he could even think what to do, John vanished. Surely James had imagined it all? Surely this was part of a dream?

The same thing happened the next night. John Jones stood by his bed, not speaking or moving. It happened each night for several weeks, always in the early hours of the morning. Then other unusual things began to occur. James heard strange noises throughout the house but could find no explanation. His belongings were moved. And the ghost of his former colleague appeared at other times of the day or night and in other places. Why was it trying to get James's attention? Did it need help?

James found this all very distressing but following the advice of his neighbours that a ghost cannot speak first but any conversation must be initiated by humans, the next time the apparition appeared he made the first move and soon learned why this sprirt was unable to rest. As his ship was passing through the notoriously rough Bay of Biscay, John Jones had fallen overboard, unnoticed by any of the crew, and drowned. This had prevented him from putting his affairs in order. Would James get his money, which was in a sea-chest stored in an inn in Plymouth - the one where they had often met - and settle his debts, in return for which he could keep what was left? Without hesitation, James agreed to undertake this one last favour. For the first time, the ghost of John Jones smiled - then vanished as before.

Next morning James set off for Plymouth, thinking all the way how he could persuade the landlady to release the chest to him. He need not have worried: John's ghost appeared again and outlined a plan. She knew them both well as regular customers; she did not know John had drowned; James should explain that John was in town and had asked James to collect his chest. Fortunately, the landlady suspected nothing and was only too pleased to oblige, indeed asking James to make sure that John came to see her again before returning to sea!

With John's ghost by his side, James cleared all the debts. When the final payment had been made John re-appeared, now looking just like his former self, younger, healthier, dressed in new clothes, just as James remembered him from when they were at sea together. The ghost thanked him and told him they would not meet again while James was alive but after he had been buried in Zennor churchyard they would once more travel the seas together.

James lived out the rest of his life in Zennor, always thinking of his friend. Just before he died an apparition appeared which everyone attending to the sick, old man saw. Soon afterwards he was buried in Zennor churchyard.

WALK DIRECTIONS

Distance 8½ miles (13.6km)   Time   4 hours
Map   OS Landranger 203 455386   Terrain This is an energetic walk. There are steep
                                              sections almost from the start and on the
                                              Coast Path, but with stretches through
                                              ancient fields and across open moorland.
Car Parking   Leave your car in Zennor village.

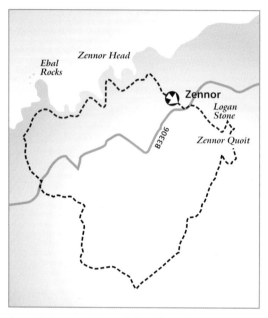

>> Take the only road signposted out of the village for car-users, past the water pump. After a few hundred yards you will meet the B3306. Turn right and then almost immediately, before the stone bridge, left down a track. When you come to a stile on your left signed 'Quoit', opposite a house called 'Eagles Nest', take the path up the hill, passing the Logan Stone on your right and going round The Carne.

>> Follow the path round to the other side of the summit to the great burial chamber of Zennor Quoit, which is on the right of your path.

This is one of the largest and most impressive Stone Age burial tombs in England, which had a barrow almost 40 feet (12m) across. Nothing remains but the inside chamber, standing as a rectangle of 5 stones plus a massive fallen capstone, the largest in Cornwall, measuring 18 feet by 11 feet (5.5m x 3.3m), and estimated to weigh 9½ tons. It is also known as Giant's Quoit and according to local lore was built by one. The stones are said to be immovable but conversely and illogically that if they are moved they will return of their own accord. In 1861 a farmer broke up one of the stones to build a cattle shed and bored holes in others before five shillings from the vicar of Zennor persuaded him to stop.

>> Follow the path until you arrive at a junction, where you turn right. Continue down, passing 'Embla Vean' on your left, and at the next junction turn right. This quickly becomes a track, on which you pass the 'Bishop's Head and Foot'.

This square stone marks the meeting point of three parishes: Zennor, Gulval and Towednack. It acquired this name because the land around here was held by the Bishop of Exeter, whose diocese covered Cornwall until relatively recently.

>> Go down to the road and walk to the T-junction. Just to the left of the telegraph pole near the car parking area, take the path which strikes straight up onto the moors. Follow this until you get to where another path crosses your's. Turn left, still ascending, and reach Mulfra Quoit. Again there are excellent views from here, as far as St Michael's Mount.

>> Do not continue on the main path but leave the summit on the west side, then swing to your right and cross a stone stile into a large field containing the Bronze Age Bodrifty Settlement, which had seven huts connected with paved walkways.

>> Leave the Settlement by crossing the stile onto the track to the west, then turn left through the metal gate. Turn right up the track, heading towards the cottage on the opposite slope. Pass in front of this cottage before going onto open moorland from the far side of the field in front of the house. Continue along this path, weaving between fields to reach Bosporthennis Farm and the path next to the stream.

>> Turn left, keeping the stream on your right, and after the last farm building on your left go diagonally uphill through three fields. Bosporthennis Quoit is in the fourth. *The unusual shape of the capstone has been attributed to giants flinging it about like a discus - but is actually the result of a local miller using it as a millstone.* Three-quarters of a mile to your left you can see Carn Galver, where the gentle Giant lived, and beyond that the hill where his friend lived.

>> Return to the path and follow the stream through several fields until you reach a stile about 60 feet in from the bank. Cross over this into the next field, then follow the path, going over more stiles until you reach a fork, with trees in front of you. Take the right hand path, crossing the stream and continuing down to the road. Here turn right and cross the bridge. The road bends to the left and just as it begins to bend to the right take the well-trodden path on your right. Go through the trees, over the stile and follow the path, passing the ruins of a mine on your right, until you emerge onto the Coast Path at the base of Gurnard's Head, with its Iron Age cliff fort, Trereen Dinas. Turn right towards Zennor.

>> Follow the Coast Path first passing Porthglaze Cove and then Pendour Cove, where the mermaid lived with Matthew Trewella, on your left, until you come to the base of Zennor Head. If you wish, you can walk round the Headland until you pick up the path again. Now cross the footbridge and take the path on your right which follows a small valley and soon joins a lane to Zennor. *In an overgrown corner of a field just to the north towards the sea is the rocking Giant's Rock (ref 454388), measuring 19 feet long by 8 feet wide (5.8m x 2.4m).*

>> Return to the lane which will take you into the village and the church on your left. *Make sure you go inside to see the carving of the mermaid. Just outside the door are three tombstones which will make you wonder about Zennor folk. They record the lives of three generations of the same family - who all lived to be over 100 years old.*

ST JUST-IN-PENWITH

THE HOOTING CARN KENIDJACK ...

Cornish miners had a tenuous hold on life. Theirs was one of permanent hardship, striving to exist alongside the likelihood of arbitrary misfortune. In 1860 children started work as young as eight years of age and conditions were so appalling that the life-expectancy of copper-miners at St Cleer was only 21. One in five workers died from accidents but the unforgiving damp, smoke-sodden air was an even greater killer and more than half died from chest complaints. Few mines boasted even the simplest form of lift and men faced the strain of climbing down two thousand feet of ladders to reach the work-face. That took three-quarters of an hour - and twice that on the return journey. Richard Couch, a mine-surgeon from St Austell, witnessed it:

> *To see the men arriving at surface after eight hours work is a most sickening sight. Thin, haggard, with arms apparently very much lengthened and hanging almost uselessly by their sides, they seem like men worn out rather than tired.*

Death and injury were commonplace. At Wheal Owles, which adjoins Botallack Mine, in 1893 miners blasted into a disused mine which had filled with water. To their horror they heard the awful sound of it rushing towards them. As a consequence of that one mistake the bodies of nineteen men and one boy are entombed forever, floating in the darkness of those deep and rocky caverns, their only memorial a plaque in St Just chapel. The tragedy at Levant in 1919 when 32 died was only the worst of many. Little wonder that the possibility of finding hidden treasure was uppermost in people's minds.

The moorland on both sides of the road from St Just-in-Penwith to Penzance is bleak, gloomy and eerie. Part of this landscape, Carn Kenidjack, is known as the 'hooting' carn because of the noise made by the wind as it whistles constantly amongst the rocky crags and piles of stones. But there is another explanation.

Late one night two miners were trudging home, having just completed a shift at the mine in Morvah. This was wage day so they stopped for a few drinks. By the time they resumed their journey it was dark, and as they approached that part of the road which passed near to Carn Kenidjack they became uneasy. They knew only too well the stories of it being the place where the Wild Hunt gathers and that mysterious sounds and lights had been heard and seen on the Carn itself. Neither had they any doubt that the dead were in possession of it.

Although there was little wind a low moaning sound came from the Carn, which quickly increased to a shriek. Nervously glancing up at the crags, the miners could see lights shining at the top and dim figures moving about. Quickening their steps they were greatly relieved to hear the sound of a horse - and even more so when they recognised it as one which worked in their mine. Now though, sitting astride was a tall man in a black cloak with a hood covering his face. Pleased to see any traveller on such a dark, bedevilled road the miners called out. In local dialect the rider replied that he was going up Carn Kenidjack to watch the wrestling, and invited them to come along, too. At that time there was nothing Cornish men-folk liked more than a good contest so, still influenced by their drink, the miners decided to see what kind of match this was which was being held in so odd a place and so late at night.

The dark rider went ahead, and when they got to the base of the hill they could see the horse picking a way among the mounds of rock, its rider beckoning them - and they noticed something else. The hooting noise from the Carn got louder and louder as they neared the top and in the dim glow they could make out the shapes of a number of men, very strange men indeed, with long, unkempt hair and painted faces gathered round an area of flat, cleared ground. By now the two miners were wishing they had gone straight home.

Dismounting, the rider threw off his cape - it was the Devil himself! Immediately, two wrestlers rushed into the clearing illuminated by fire from the eyes of the spectating demons. The wrestlers were very skilful, the contest was even and fought vigorously until finally one lifted the other high into the air and flung him against a boulder in a back fall. The rocks shook and the land groaned with the force. The spectators crowded round the winner. No one moved to help the stricken loser. The miners were askance: how could they let their companion lie hurt, possibly seriously, after such a good performance?

Both miners were compassionate men and one who had been a lay preacher bent down to comfort the injured wrestler by gently whispering a few words of the Lord's Prayer to him. The effect was immediate and shattering. It was as if a thunderbolt had fallen. The rocks shook, the whole moorland became enveloped in a black cloud, there was the noise of a great rushing wind, and the earth pulsated beneath the terrified miners' quivering feet. When this violent outburst had passed all the fiendish assembly had disappeared: painted men, dying man and Devil, as well as the wrestling ring. Gone. The two miners crouched, trembling, as over their heads passed a pair of terrible, flaming eyes which disappeared, with a hoot.

The pair spent what was left of the night stumbling around Carn Kenidjack trying to find their way off the hill but, lost and exhausted, there they remained until in the welcome light of dawn they were able to make their way home. What an escape. Are you surprised that we prefer to come here in broad daylight - never after dark?

... WHERE THERE ARE KNOCKERS ...

Not only were the carns around here swarming with creatures of the nether world but, as if the tinners did not have enough to contend with in their harsh lives, the mines themselves were alive with the knockers. The sounds of their little picks could be heard at almost every level. Here in the mines around St Just they were particularly fractious and spiteful.

One of the tinners from St Just, Tom Trevorrow, was as sceptical as any of their powers. He had heard from more experienced miners how the *bucca*, the knockers, liked to be left pieces of *fuggan*, lardy cake, from the miners' meals, but took no notice. He worked in Bollowall Mine and one day heard the little creatures talking there, but instead of respecting their presence told them to be quiet and go away. Immediately he was struck with a fall of small stones. Unconcerned, he continued working. After a short while the knockers spoke again, "*Tom Trevorrow! Tom Trevorrow! Leave some of thy fuggan for Bucca or bad luck to thee tomorrow.*" Again Tom shouted at them to go away - or he would knock their brains out! The knockers' mood changed. They repeated their request but now their voices were louder, harder, harsher, emphasising their threat of bad luck.

And they kept their word. When Tom arrived at work next day he found that a rock-fall had buried not only his precious tools but also the lode of rich ore he had been digging to provide his month's wages. Tom though was not disheartened. He carried on, hoping his luck would change, but it never did. On the contrary it went from bad to worse until he was forced to leave the mine and become a farm labourer - a miserable exchange for a tinner.

At another mine nearby, Ransom Mine, the knockers were particularly active, concentrating at a level known as 'the Bockles'. All the miners believed that this is were the richest lodes could be found but none dared to work it for fear of offending the creatures. One night around midnight an old miner called Trenwith, who lived near Bosprenis, was with his son in the mine when they actually saw the knockers dragging out great heaps of shining ore. Carefully, respectfully and apprehensively, the Trenwiths spoke to them. They had in mind an agreement. In exchange for being allowed to work the lode they would at the end of each day leave one tenth of the most valuable metal ore, properly prepared, to save the knockers the trouble of having to toil through every night. The knockers agreed. While he was working the old man stuck strictly to the arrangement, never once failing to leave the knockers their share. Despite leaving one tenth of the best ore he still earned twice as much money as any other tinner at Ransom, and soon grew wealthy. When he died though his son had other ideas. He was more selfish, and had little respect for the knockers. He continued to work at 'the Bockles' but reneged on the agreement, keeping all the ore he dug for himself and left none behind. It wasn't long before the knockers reacted. The lode failed, the rich veins ran out. The young man received no more help from the knockers. It wasn't long before he had to leave the mine but could find no alternative employment. In desperation he took to drink, squandered everything left by his father, and when he himself died was buried as a pauper.

Do you need any further evidence of the knockers' powers?

... AND FAIRIES ON THE GUMP ...

The Gump, or more correctly Woon Gumpus Common, is a windswept, treeless, uninhabited area between Morvah and St Just. Over this desolate heath the Devil hunts lost souls, catching them at an old stile over which no-one ever escapes. It is also a favourite playground of one branch of the Small Folk, the piskeys. Here they hold their festivals - and woe betide any human who spies on them!

Unfortunately, some human beings can be very greedy, and one bright moonlit night around harvest time an old man surreptitiously made his way towards the Gump. He had been planning this trip for a long time and knew just what he was looking for. As he got near he heard fairy music, then with a tremendous crash the whole area opened up in front of him and out marched a crowd of piskeys. Lanterns hung from every blade of grass, furze bushes twinkled with stars, the tiny green lights of glow-worms lit the way. Musicians were followed by servants carrying tables, silver plates, gold cups, baskets of food and platters of cakes. Finally came thousands of brightly dressed men and women, singing exquisitely for their fairy Prince and Princess. The old man was unmoved. He had eyes only for their treasure.

The festival began with ceremonial marching up and down the Gump. The old man crouched down to avoid being seen. Stealthily he crept to a mound and then began to crawl on his stomach. He peeped over - and thousands of pairs of little eyes stared back at him. All in stony silence. He snatched off his hat and put it over the fairy Prince and Princess intending to make off with them as well as the treasure but with a piercing whistle his hand was transfixed in mid-air. He couldn't move it. The piskeys had of course seen what was going on and had thrown invisible threads around him. His whole body ached as they pinched and punched him. He couldn't get up from the ground and even his tongue was tied so he was unable to utter a single sound. To add further embarrassment one little piskey stood on his nose, making it hurt as if he had been stung.

Fortunately for him it wasn't long before he heard a shout: "*Away, away, I smell the day.*" The Small Folk disappeared leaving the old man alone on the Gump with only his thoughts - and his bruises. As the sun rose he found he had been held by myriads of gossamer webs, now glistening in the early morning dew. He was wet, cold, hungry and ashamed at what he had done. Shaking himself free he went home with less spring in his step than when he had left it hours earlier. He never told anyone where he had spent that night. So when you visit the Gump we suggest you do so in daytime - but if you insist on going after dark be aware that it really is the territory of the piskeys.

... AS WELL AS A GHOST...

Pendeen has one of the finest cliff-scapes in Cornwall. At the bottom is Pendeen Cave which some believe stretches to the Scilly Isles, though the entrance is now blocked up. John Lenine was a local smuggler who used Pendeen Cave as his landing base and brought his goods along the subterranean passage to Pendeen House.

That is where Avis Penkivell lived with her father. She was a haughty, conceited, self-obsessed young lady, sufficiently attractive to have several potential suitors calling to see her but was more interested in hunting than such a trifling matter as being courted. One young man, her cousin John Lenine, was more determined than the rest and on his smuggling journeys to France bought her all sorts of finery, silks and laces. But despite the risks he was taking for her, the progress of his courting was slow. Eventually though, Avis agreed to marry him - provided he brought her, on Christmas Day, a red rose.

Off John went in search of red roses. As he sailed out of Pendeen Bay he didn't notice that a large naval vessel was positioning itself below the cliffs; nor did he know that the captain was under strict orders to arrest him. You see, behind John's back, Avis had met and become very fond of the captain, and in their whisperings had told him about the hidden passage from the Cave - for after all if she kept the captain up to date with John's movements, he might himself be inclined to marry her. In the meantime John had been to Nice and bought a rose bush which would bloom on Christmas Day, then returned still unaware of the trap. Christmas Day arrived and John set off to claim his promised bride. Just as he got to the secret door into Pendeen House he was seized by the ship's crew. He put up a tremendous struggle, holding his red rose in his hand and fighting like fury, until both he and the captain lay injured, side by side, on the sands - and now heard of Avis Penkivell's deceit.

With his last breath the captain ordered the ship's boy to take the rose to Avis with the message that she could now wear it in triumph - for both he and her lover were dead. Avis Penkivell was shunned by every man for miles around and from the day she died her ghost has haunted these parts, still carrying a red rose.

... AND MORE FAIRIES.

Grace Treva lived with her parents on a small-holding near the foot of Carn Kenidjack. It was a hard existence, barely beyond a subsistence level. For most of the time Grace didn't seem to mind until in her mid-teens she was persuaded by a cousin to go into service. For the first time in her young life Grace would have to go more than a day's journey from her village. With her meagre bundle of belongings she set off walking past Carn Kenidjack, where as a youngster she had played for many happy hours, memories which brought tears to her eyes. She was though a determined girl. As she was drying her eyes with her apron she saw a gentleman standing close to her. He was a widower, he told her, and had come to find 'a tidy maid' to look after his house and his son. Grace could have the job if she wanted. Now that was a stroke of good luck!

Grace did wonder how he knew her name but he spoke so kindly that she was not in the least reluctant to go with him. They set off, walking always downhill through the most attractive countryside. She had no idea of the distance they had covered. Time just flew by and it was almost sunset before they arrived at her new master's house, hidden by roses and flowering plants spread over its walls and roof. In the kitchen a wood fire blazed, and on a stool sat a prim, sour-looking woman, knitting. Her eyes bore into Grace. Then in bounded the young son to see his father, and though he was only as tall as a six- or seven-year-old his face was like an old man's. He looked at Grace just like the old woman, as sharp, cunning and hostile.

Grace went about her chores and Prudence, the old woman, gave her details of her duties and warnings of certain things she must never, ever do. By the time she had eaten, Grace had forgotten about her home, parents, siblings and friends. By bedtime her thoughts were focussed only on her kind master and the delightful place they lived in.

Grace's new life was so pleasant that months passed like a single day, but she was an adventurous young girl, energetic and inquisitive, and soon became bored with only the hens for company. That led her into trouble.

Grace became curious about the things she had been warned against, particularly about certain locked private rooms. When her opportunity came she nipped inside - and to her horror saw men's heads, torsoes and arms on shelves and in cupboards while over the fireplace were whole bodies of small people, all turned to white stone, just as she had heard in old folks' tales. Grace stepped backwards to leave - and bumped into a furious Aunt Prudence who ordered her to help polish the furniture. Grace rubbed away so hard she jerked a long dark chest off its frame. Something inside groaned, which disturbed her master. Now he was angry as she had disobeyed instructions - next time she must beware!

It was many days before her master returned to his normal self, but having seen inside that room worried Grace: she could not understand this place and its inhabitants. One evening Grace could hear the unmistakeable sounds of a banquet. She crept down the staircase and peeped through the partly-open of the door of the room private and was rivetted by a fair-haired lady sitting by the long box and thumping it until whatever was inside gave out the finest music Grace had ever heard.

In the morning when her master came in Grace confronted him: he wasn't a human being but a changeling and an enchanter. He knew straight away that she had disobeyed him again. Now they must part. Grace pleaded to stay but her master would not reconsider.

Next day she packed her bags. She was heart-broken, but at daybreak set off on the back of her master's horse. They cantered through the lanes, going uphill all the time but in what seemed just a few minutes Grace recognised Carn Kenidjack. Without a word, her master stopped and put her on the rock where he had first seen her. Grace lay down and wept. Not until nightfall did she walk slowly over the downs to her parents' cottage.

The old folks were surprised to see her as she had been given up long ago. Though Grace's story seemed strange, those who knew about these things concluded that one of the changeling small people must have carried her away to his house in a wood, and there she had lived the full nine years as every-one else in her position was required to do - even though they had seemed less than one to her. Moreover, Grace had changed. She couldn't settle. She couldn't get on with her parents or brothers and sisters. She disliked their poverty. She couldn't work with any regularity. She took no interest in her clothes or money. Yet within less than two years she had married a widower who had been left with several small children, and when she recovered fully people said it was the hard work which had cured her. But she never forgot her life away from the Carn.

WALK DIRECTIONS

Distance   11½ miles (18.5km)   Time   6 hours
Map   OS Landranger 203   370313 Terrain There are some steep climbs on the Coast
                                               Path and   some walking across open
                                               moorland.
Car Parking   Park in the main square at St Just.

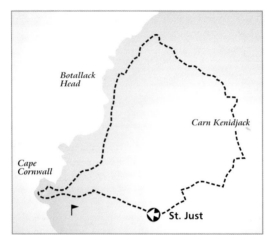

The road which runs down the north coast between St Ives and Land's End passes through this old mining village. An unkind eighteenth-century visitor described it as "a sad, dismal place, situated in a most inhospitable and cheerless corner of the county." But there is something different about it, something mystical. It could be its location between the wild Atlantic and the rugged moors. It could be its long history as the centre of mining history that brought such prosperity but much loss and sorrow. It could be that it is surrounded by relics of a people long gone.

>>   From the car park cross the road and turn right, walking to the end of the row of terraced houses on your left. Turn left into the Plen-an-Gwary.
     This circular amphitheatre was used in the Middle Ages to stage Mystery Plays and athletic competitions. Later, visiting Methodists preached in it. Once ringed by six stone steps of benches it may be even older than thought as, intriguingly, the entrance is aligned with the summer solstice sunrise.

>>   Leave at the clock tower, cross the road and turn left into Boswedden Road. At the crossroads continue straight ahead. At the corner of the school, where the road bears right continue straight ahead down the lane and the footpath to Boswedden. Here, turn left between the buildings and right at the road before continuing down to Cape Cornwall.

>>   From the Cape go uphill past the car park to a granite wall on your left where a waymark indicates the Coast Path and Pendeen Watch. Turn left, ignore the wide path on your right and continue straight ahead on the narrower track which leads inland. Pass a pond on your left as you head towards the large chimney stack. At the T-junction, bear left and follow the track over the stream, emerging on to a lane below a cottage. Turn left. Just past the end of the cottage's garden wall turn right, going uphill, to arrive at the Coast Path.

This section has the most stunning views, facing the full might of the Atlantic. Advances in hard rock mining and engineering technologies during the eighteenth and nineteenth centuries drastically altered the landscape, economy and society of the region, placing it at the forefront of the Industrial Revolution. Distinctive physical reminders of this past persist. You will pass the remains of several old engine-houses, some perched precariously yet romantically on the cliffs. Their shafts ran under the sea and in stormy conditions the miners could hear the sounds of boulders grinding, rumbling and rolling about on the seabed just a few yards above their heads. The redness of the sea is another legacy of the industry - it is caused by waste from the mines. The unnatural red and green colours of the rocks are further reminders of its environmental effects.

>> Follow the Coast Path, winding through the ruins of Levant Mine on your left, where even the buildings are stained red, and continue downhill to the stream and footbridge at Levant Zawn.

The settling beds are still full of red mud and the waste from Geevor Mine is carried to the sea by the stream. Geevor was one of the last to close after the price of tin slumped in the 1980s.

>> Cross the footbridge and after about 50 yards (45m) turn right inland where it is waymarked. Pendeen House Farm lies to your north. When this path meets the road take the right fork, continuing ahead to the corner shop in Pendeen. Cross this road (B3306), turn left and almost immediately right up St John's Terrace.

>> Very soon this narrow road becomes a track on which you pass a small wood before emerging onto the road (B3318). The expanse of Woon Gumpus Common is over to your left. Turn right and at the next minor road on your right look for the milestone to Tewellard and St Just, where you again turn right. After about 50 yards (45m) turn left onto a walled farm track just before the 'Slow' marking on the road.

>> Stay on this walled track until when it turns left towards the farm buildings you continue straight ahead towards four telegraph poles. Just after these poles you will emerge onto the moor at Wheal Bal Hill. To visit Carn Kenidjack follow the track straight ahead of you: you can see the Carn's fantastic rock shapes on the skyline. This becomes a narrower bridle path and leads directly to the top.

Of course, if you are very brave you can climb at night and hear the strange noises and see unexplained lights on top of the Carn.

>> Return to the edge of the moor and continue downhill. At the bottom turn right across Carnyorth Common, passing Tregeseal Stone Circle on your left.

This Bronze Age circle is the only remaining one of three which were here. Like so many others they were vandalised partly by digging a quarry, partly by the stones being used for building. Now only 10 of the original 17 stones remain.

At the next junction of paths, with a waymark on your right and a pond straight ahead, turn left along a lane, passing farm buildings.

>> At the T-junction turn right. The lane soon becomes a narrow metalled road which you follow as it winds downhill to the stream. Cross the wooden footbridge on your left and continue straight ahead on the public footpath behind the houses until you reach the road. Here, turn left and after 100 yards (90m) turn right up a footpath, passing the church and arriving at the square in St Just. The car park is straight ahead on the road to the library.

TREGESEAL

THE PIRATE-WRECKER

There is an old saying which was very apposite to this part of Cornwall: *"Ask not, sailor, whose body lies here. I wish you better luck than mine, and a kindlier sea."* Many victims of shipwreck ended their lives on this savage coastline, with its notorious reefs, conflicting tides and changing currents and their gravestones are catalogued in nearby churchyards. A substantial proportion fell victim to the Brisons, those fearsome, menacing twin rocks which jut defiantly above the creaming, foaming waters a mile or so to the south-west of Cape Cornwall. Worst of all was to strike the reef between the Brisons, where the force could snap masts and split timbers as the heartrending screams of crew and frightened passengers went unheard in the cacophony of wind and wave.

But the sea stirs our blood, especially when we are assailed with stories of how local wreckers lured ships onto rocks with false lights on the cliffs. In reality this was an invention of Victorian novelists. 'Wrecking' to the local population consisted of stripping an already stricken vessel of all useful articles, as contributions to their livelihood. None, even in the direst poverty, would deliberately lure ships onto rocks. That didn't stop local clergy praying *"not that there will be wrecks, O Lord, but that if they be, then that they be sent ashore here to the benefit of the poor inhabitants."* At another time a St Just child made the plea, *"God bless Vaather 'n' Mawther, 'n' zend a ship t'shore vore mornin'"* Then again there was a wreck here on a Sunday just as the villagers were trooping into church. As the vicar's sermon droned on interminably the restless congregation looked anxiously to see if the weather was breaking up and with it the rich remains of the wreck. The last hymn was sung and as the vicar began his final blessing he wrenched off his surplice and sprinted down the aisle shouting, *"Now we all start fair ..."* But read on ...

One autumn evening many years ago a ship headed for the coast off the western tip of Cornwall, the skull and crossbones flying at her masthead. A large crowd gathered to watch from the shelter of Carn Gloose, becoming increasingly alarmed as it headed their way. It stopped, anchors were lowered and a small boat pulled away carrying a man pinned in chains. The oarsmen rowed quickly into Priest's Cove where the man was made to stand at gunpoint, his chains removed and he was thrown into the deep water. As he scrambled ashore the watchers heard him shrieking curses at the sailors now heading back. He was a pirate so evil that even his own crew had rejected him and thrown him off his ship.

In almost no time at all the man had bought a small farm at Tregeseal and settled into the cottage. Before very long local folk began to wonder why so many ships foundered on the cliffs bordering his farm. To their horror they discovered that he had not been farming at all but was luring passing ships onto the rocks. His method was simple but effective: after fastening his horse's head to one foreleg, he would tie a lantern round its neck then whip it along the clifftops after dark. In poor visibility ships' look-outs quite reasonably but tragically interpreted this moving light as the stern of another ship seeking shelter and that they would reach safety and deep water if they steered straight for it - until they hit the rocks.

Anyone surviving, crew and passengers alike, were treated with inhuman savagery: even if they reached land the pirate-wrecker showed them no mercy, staving in their skulls with an axe or cutting off their hands as they tried to grasp the rocky ledges along the shore. Dozens of ships were torn to pieces in this way - until he grew old and became terminally ill.

It was one of those calm, windless Autumn evenings at harvest time. Two men mowing barley in a field near the pirate-wrecker's cottage felt a sudden breeze ruffling through the crop and heard a strange voice whisper breathlessly, *"The hour is nigh but the man isn't come."* The breeze blew stronger and as the men looked towards the horizon, the Isles of Scilly clearly silhouetted against the sky, they noticed a square-rigged ship, her black sails set, bearing smoothly in towards the Cape against the prevailing wind and tide. There was no sign of her crew or anyone on board. As she moved a swirl of darkness gathered around her. Still she came on until the tops of her masts were close against the cliffs. The dense black clouds rose across the fields and descended precisely onto the cottage where the dying pirate-wrecker lay. The farm workers had seen enough. They abandoned their work and fled to Tregeseal. A crowd of frightened neighbours had already gathered outside the cottage, waiting silently for the priest.

Inside the cottage was a different scenario. The room was filled with the sound of a rushing sea and the terrified screams of the dying man. He called for clergymen to save him from the devils and from the sailors he had killed, who had now returned to tear him to pieces. Here was a changed man: no longer arrogantly confident but writhing in paroxysms of agony and terror, *"The devil is tearing at me with nails like the claws of a hawk! Put out the sailors with their bloody hands! The flames are licking round me even now."*

As soon as they arrived the priest and the doctor went into the room, but only to be cursed for their concern. The sound of the sea grew louder, the black cloud from the ship came into the cottage, the room trembled with a dull throb until an enormous clap of thunder and flash of lightning shook the very ground itself. Not knowing if this was an earthquake or if the cottage had been engulfed by waves or fiendish devils, the priest and the doctor rushed outside. The storm unleashed its fury over the wrecker's cottage - then as suddenly as it had come the wraith-like haze rolled back and wrapped itself around the ship which glided away amongst flashes of lightning and deafening thunderclaps. The villagers were awe-struck.

With more than trepidation, the priest returned to find the pirate-wrecker dead, his eyes staring at some unseen thing, his face set in a ghastly expression of sheer terror. A coffin was hastily knocked together, the wrecker's body placed inside, the lid sealed - but as it was being hurried to the churchyard other unearthly events occurred. First, a black pig joined the procession but evaporated into thin air as suddenly as it had come. Then as the cortege approached the church the sky grew darker and another violent thunderstorm blew up. The bearers dropped the coffin onto the stile and fled into the porch for shelter and safety as the elements raged about them. From nowhere a shaft of light, more brilliant even than the lightning, struck the coffin which burst into flames before whirling into the air and out to sea, tossing wildly in the violent wind in the wake of the black-sailed ship. When the storm abated all that was left of the coffin were the handles and a few nails. The black pig was never seen again. Nor the death ship.

WALK DIRECTIONS

Distance   5 miles (8.2km)   Time   2½ hours
Map   OS Landranger 203 370313 Terrain Moderate along roads, paths and the Coast
                                              Path, with two modest climbs on the latter.
Car Parking   Park in the main square in St Just

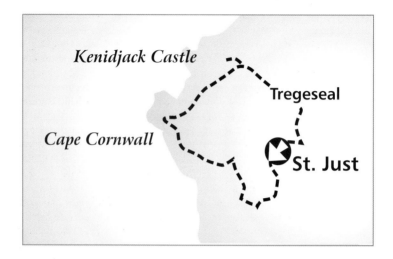

>> With the Fire Station and Library on your right, turn left and take the road out of town, which soon becomes 'Unsuitable For Motors'. Walk on and at the end of this road go over the stile, keeping the wall on your right until you go over another stile onto an enclosed path which leads you to a lane.

>> Here turn right and at the fork bear right again, passing the youth hostel on your left. Where the road bends right you turn left and then sharply right. At the junction turn right again and across the footbridge over the stream. At the road turn left, heading towards the sea and walk along the Cot valley.

>> Take the first track to your right and go up the cliff to join the road.
The chimney to your right is a remnant of the former Bollowall Mine, which provided the story of Tom Trevorrow, who was rude to the knockers and suffered as a consequence. Just over the road, also on your right, is Bollowall Barrow, the largest in Cornwall and a fine example of dry-stone masonry. Probably dating from the Bronze Age (1500-500 BC) it is as impressive as its setting.
The metalled road soon becomes a stony track as you descend to Cape Cornwall.
This is the only Cape in England. The old mine stack that tops it is a striking piece of industrial archaeology, standing on a low headland to your left and overlooking the shingle beach at Priest's Cove. Erected in 1850 it served the boiler of the beam winder of Cape Cornwall Mine, which though never a real success worked for a period of about forty years until it was finally 'knacked' in the 1870s.

>> At the track junction turn left and go down to Priest's Cove.
This little cove is where the wicked pirate's ship put in and from where the death ship set sail when he died. Has it retained its uncanny atmosphere?

Actually it had nothing to do with priests. Its name derives from Porth Just, pronounced 'Jeest' in earlier times, before becoming corrupted to 'Porth East' and eventually distorted further into 'Priest's'. In the days when the mines were in production Priest's Cove sheltered the fishing boats belonging to miners, who spent any spare time supplementing their diet and income.

>> Turn right and climb up the road, with the car park on your right, and at the Coast Path waymark turn left, still ascending with the wall to your right. At the fork, bear right and follow the Path inland above a small valley. Keep on the Coast Path and descend to a footbridge over the Tregeseal stream. At the houses turn left along the track until you reach a signpost and stile on your right. Go over and climb to a track where you turn left towards the sea but at the next Coast Path waymark turn right to the ruined building at the top on your left.

From here you can explore Kenidjack Cliff Castle, but then retrace your steps.

Walk past the Rifle Club on your right and keep on the Coast Path to its junction with a broad, stony track, where you turn right.

>> Now you are going inland and soon reach a metalled road, signed 'Nancherrow'. *The area is now quiet, the rush and roar and fumes of its mines has gone, the thump of ore-crushing tin stamps no more. All you can hear are the birds. In 1822, in the short distance between Bostraze and the sea, this stream turned the wheels of no less than 17 stamp-mills and 3 grist-mills.*

The larger hamlet you can see beyond is Tregeseal. Go into Nancherrow and at the road junction turn right, signed 'St Just'. Turn right and cross the bridge, then left and up the steps onto a footpath. This bears right up a field to a stile and onto a path heading towards St Just church, whose tower you can now see on the horizon.

>> Cross three fields with stiles until you reach an enclosed path past the church. *St Just church contains the gravestone of Selus, who may possibly have been the son of Gereint, a local ruler in the sixth century, and brother of Iestyn whose name was Latinised into 'Just'.*

Continue along the road into the square and your car.

BOSULLOW COMMON

LEGENDS OF THE STONES

Everywhere you walk in Cornwall the landscape is punctuated by prehistoric structures. The moors are rich with remains of haunting Neolithic burial chambers and megalithic quoits while Bronze Age ceremonial sites survive in stone circles. Along the coastline lie the visible remnants of Iron Age forts guarded seaward by savage cliffs and landward by great mounds of earth and stone. From a later age, the so-called Dark Ages, come many of the inscribed standing stones and old crosses. Archaeology can tell us little about the ancient people who struggled against the elements with few tools to build them. But their spirit casts its spell.

Madron Moor is small compared to Bodmin Moor but is just as heavy with history. It feels as if every field contains an old stone relic of some kind. Less than a mile from the Trevowhan-Madron road, two upright stone pillars flank a circular one which has an almost perfect round hole through its centre. This is Men-an-Tol. Its history is obscure and it is difficult to understand just what function this unusual assembly served for the Bronze Age men who erected them 4,000 years ago. Could its original purpose have been astronomical, to mark the sunrise in May and August and the sunset in February and November, the Celtic quarter days? Or from time immemorial did the central holed stone hold mystical, magical properties associated with fertility? Or was it used to control some natural power of which we have lost all knowledge? Certainly it has been credited with therapeutic powers. Local people believed that crawling through would cure their ailments and mothers of unwell children passed - dragged, more likely - them naked through the narrow hole '*trice against the sun*', then rubbed them on the grass as a cure for scrofula and rickets, which vanished miraculously under the stone's influence. Adult sufferers were not neglected. Those with spinal disorders, rheumatism or sciatica crawled on all fours round the central stone before creeping through the hole. Try it and see if it works! Maybe it is a universal panacea! Then again, engaged couples would come and hold hands through the hole to ensure a long and happy marriage with lots of children. And that is not all. The stone has prophetic qualities, too. Lay two brass pins across each on the top of the holed stone or hang them by a thread, and some latent force will answer any question you ask: the way they turn, move and point all have a deep mysterious and meaningful significance. And who are we to say ...?

Throughout Cornwall there are stories of secret gold hidden beneath ancient monuments. The Men Scryfa, from the Cornish 'stone of writing', only a short walk from the Men-an-Tol, is one of them. This impressive pillar is unusual in that on the north side is a faintly carved Latin inscription dating from the early Dark Ages, written about a thousand years after it was first erected and thought to mark the burial place of a king or chieftain slain in the battle of Goon-adga-idniall on Gendhal Moor. It bears the words *Rialobrani Cunovali Filii*, 'Rialobran son of Cunoval'. Folklore tells us that this king, the 'Royal Raven', stood nine feet tall, the same height as the stone, and that he lies beneath with all his weapons and treasures. This seems unlikely, but one nineteenth-century local decided to put this to the test, despite it having stood here for two thousand years. He had dreamt that a crock of gold was buried underneath the stone and eventually dug a pit around its base. He didn't find gold but he and so many others have tried that the pillar actually fell down, lying forlornly until in 1862 the Antiquarian Society replaced it in its rightful position over the warrior's grave.

Prosaic archaeologists consider that the megalithic dolmens or cromlechs are the bare remains of prehistoric burial chambers, erected up to 4,000 years ago by Stone Age people for the families of their priestly chiefs. Folklore will always ignore the expert and tells us they are really quoits used by playful giants in their favourite game of 'bob-button', and whose fingers created the recesses in them. Giants certainly lived around here for near Boscawen-Un are two of their footprints and nearby pillars mark their graves.

Half a mile from Men-an-Tol is Lanyon Quoit, its massive capstone supported by three smaller pillars. In profile it has such a close resemblance to a table that, presumably when the giants had tired of it, lore tells us a group of Saxon kings used it as their dining table, amongst whom was King Arthur on the eve of his last battle. Merlin came here too, and prophesied that Arthur and his chieftains would gather again just before the end of the world.

WALK DIRECTIONS

Distance 4½ miles (7.1km)   Time   2 hours
Map   OS Landranger 203 418344 Terrain The walking is easy to moderate,
                                             mostly moorland with a few gentle climbs.
Car Parking   Park in the lay-by opposite the Men-an-Tol Print Studio.

>>   Take the broad track which leads inland across the moors, signed 'Men-an-Tol and Men Scryfa'. Initially, you will walk between high stone walls which border the traditionally small fields of Penwith, passing on your left a barn built with gigantic stones - surely only a giant could have raised them from the ground? - but the moorland soon opens out.

This is part of the ancient Tinners' Way from Sennen to St Ives along which early traders collected tin and copper from moorland smelting works.

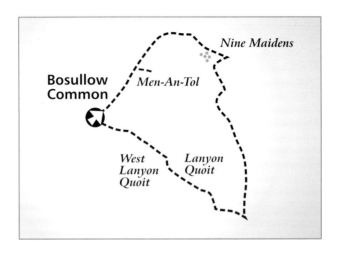

>> After about 15 minutes along the track the Men-an-Tol stands just to your right, through the heather and gorse. After inspecting it, and you feel you have been cured, return to the track and continue for about 400 yards until you to reach a junction of several paths. To visit Men Scryfa turn left. You will see it in a field straight ahead, in front of a rocky tor, and can reach it by crossing the stone stile over the wall. Again, return to the track and continue to the next junction of paths, having passed a ruined cottage on your left.
Nearby is a large 'whale-back' rock with a cross-hole carved in it. This is 'Four Parishes', the orginal meeting place of the ancient parishes of Morvah, Madron, Zennor and Gulval; the cross-hole marks the actual parish boundaries.

>> You now leave the shelter of stone walls and at the junction of several paths across the moors take the right hand one leading east uphill to the stone circle of Boskednan. Don't confuse the first group of stones you pass on your left with the Nine Maidens circle: they are part of the chamber of a Bronze Age barrow. The stone circle, one of four in Cornwall known as 'Nine Maidens', is a few minutes' walk further on. Its location has retained its atmospheric mystery.
A Bronze Age monument of the period 2,000-1,500 BC, the circle probably had 20-22 upright stones spaced round a circle of about 25 yards, but now there are only seven. Writing in the 1750s, Dr Borlase discovered 13 stones and also described a single menhir off to the north-west. It is one of only two true circles in the Penwith area, the other three being more eliptical.

>> Continue along the path, making for a derelict engine house on the horizon of the hill, which has been called "the most romantic deserted mine in the country." When you reach a pot-holed track turn right and meander through the heather.
Greenburrow was the pumping house for the Ding Dong Mine where Richard Trevethick worked. Its shafts and tunnels spread like tentacles beneath the surrounding moorland, reaching a depth of 815 feet (247m). The mine has been worked from the early Dark Ages (young for an area which has been mined for

4,000years) but the present ruins belong to one which opened in 1814.
From the mine you can see the rocky Carn Galver where Giant Holiburn lived.
It also affords a panoramic view across the moors to Mount's Bay.
>> The rough track soon joins a metalled roadway with Bosiliak Farm on your right. Continue along this until you join the road from Madron village. Here, turn right.
>> As this road twists left and then begins to descend, go over the stone stile on your right and cross the fields in front of Pontshallow. In about half a mile you will see Lanyon Quoit on your right. You can go up to it over steps in the wall.

This is a good example of a Stone Age long barrow burial chamber, though it has been extensively altered and rebuilt over the ages. Stone Age people buried their dead tribal chieftains in such tombs, created by hoisting a huge flat capstone to balance on stone uprights, and then covered the whole mound with earth and turf to make a barrow. The feat, work and skill of these early people is almost beyond belief. Dr Borlase wrote in 1754 that the quoit was so high that a man could ride underneath the capstone on horseback, which was then supported by four pillars. But thousands of years of standing came to an end when the whole lot collapsed in a fierce storm on 19 October 1815, breaking one of the stone supports. The quoit was re-assembled in 1824 but with the uprights deeper into the ground and the capstone, which had also been broken, supported on three remaining pillars. Stand and wonder how this 13-ton capstone was raised 5,000 tears ago!

>> Continue along this road passing Lanyon Farm, behind which is another dolmen, West Lanyon Quoit. Very shortly you will reach your car.

SENNEN

OF SMUGGLERS AND SPIRITS ...

The old mansion at Penrose no longer exists. Centuries ago it stood at the head of a lonely valley east of Sennen through which a stream ran to Penberth Cove, its pointed gables and massive chimney-stacks looking out over ivy-covered walls, courtyards and gardens. Now a Georgian farmhouse occupies the site. Within a generation, successive sons died without heir until the property devolved onto one of the two youngest, Ralph. He was only marginally interested in it but more so in a fast, locally-built, well-armed smuggling ship which was captained by his cousin, William Penrose. Together they crossed to France and other places smuggling wines, spirits, tobacco - anything from which they could evade customs duties - spending little time on shore. When his wife died unexpectedly, Ralph was heartbroken. He spent even more time at sea, taking his seven-year-old son and leaving the youngest brother, Jan, and a bailiff to look after the estate and farms. However, returning from one of his trips one dark, cold winter's night, their heavily-laden boat struck a rock on Cowloe Reef. Ralph swam into Sennen Cove with his son but was drowned while trying to save his crew.

Jan became guardian of the boy and effectively master of Penrose. At first he seemed attentive to the orphaned heir, and he too bought a large smuggling ship but his crew were different. In a regime of piracy the captain and men boarded many a rich merchantman going up the Channel, took whatever they pleased and sent everything - and everyone - else to the bottom of the sea. One winter's night Jan's men joined the neighbourhood hunting for a wolf which was devastating local flocks of sheep and had been sighted on Sennen's cliffs, but neither he nor his captain went. When the hunters returned the young boy did not come to meet them, as he always had done. An extensive search revealed no trace. The child must have missed his way returning from Sennen Cove where he had spent much of his time after his father had drowned there, wandered out under Escols Cliff, and been drowned himself.

Now Jan showed his profligate, reckless nature. He gambled away much of the estate. His captain left. The north wing of the house was emptied and acquired the reputation of being haunted.

The following Christmas-time Jan Penrose arranged a large party at Penrose. Every-one was enjoying the evening's activities when an elderly traveller arrived at the door, seeking shelter from a storm. Jan agreed and left the steward to make the arrangements, though the only spare accommodation was in the north wing. The stranger was in no hurry to settle down and spent a long time examining the old portraits. By midnight the storm had lessened, and in the bright moonlight he could see a silent procession of young men and women passing through the courtyard: he knew they were going to gather ivy and set it alight, enabling them to see into the future, and foretell especially the most important events in their lives, marriage and death. He had not been sitting long however when the group came running back, apparently in great fright. The doors slammed, the music stopped. Within a moment the house was shrouded in dense swirling fog. All was still. Then came a noise like the sea roaring in the distance, though that was a mile and a half away. The sound got closer and in the wailing wind could be heard the noise of oars in their rowlocks, and the hollow voices of the smugglers who had been drowned with the old Squire, years earlier. It was some time before the sounds died away but not before Ralph's face appeared to the watching stranger, calling in a familiar voice, "*William Penrose, arise and avenge the murder of thy cousin's son!*" The man was indeed William Penrose. By some miracle he had survived the shipwreck. Looking towards the window he saw a boy dressed all in white: it was the lost heir of Penrose. Coming nearer, the spirit told how he had been murdered by the captain of the pirate-smugglers on the day the others were hunting; how he had been buried in a shallow grave under an apple tree in the orchard; how the murderer was now in Plymouth, the landlord of a public house; how the spirit would only find peace if his body were exhumed and re-buried in consecrated ground at Sennen churchyard.

Early next morning William Penrose left Penrose for Plymouth, where he found the public house exactly as the apparition had described. Though the landlord was much the worse for drink, William Penrose initiated a conversation, talking of Sennen, then of Penrose, then of an apple tree which he described in detail. The man was horrified. He begged for mercy and confessed how for a long time he had hated the boy's parents and how he had acted only on Jan's instructions to remove the one obstacle to ownership of the estate. But what possible motive could this man ever have for such feelings about the Squire and his wife? The publican continued: he was the son of an old family whose home was within a few miles of Penrose. In his younger days he loved - and was loved by - a local lady and had left home to become a privateer so he could make enough money to impress the lady's parents. But Ralph Penrose had wooed and won the lady for whom he had borne such considerable hardship and risk over many years. He wanted revenge. He bought a fast sailing ship and for several more years roamed the seas, evolving a plan to carry the lady off to some foreign land. One night he and his crew landed at Whitesand Bay and made their way to Penrose - to hear that the lady had been buried just a few days before. Again he took to sea but his ship foundered on Gwenvor Sands and he lost everything. When drunk he had agreed to Jan's scheme in return for gold. Since then he had never had a single moment free from remorse.

William returned to Penrose and with the steward and other staff removed the child's remains from underneath the apple tree, re-interring them in Sennen churchyard. That same night Jan Penrose hanged himself in the old mansion. Not surprisingly, his ghost haunted it for a long time afterwards. William Penrose's task was not yet completed. Next day he and his helpers found the bodies of the old Squire and his crew in the moist sand near Gwenvor Cove, exactly where fishermen had seen corpse lights and heard drowned sailors 'hailing their names', seeking help from the living. Their remains were laid to rest near Chapel Idne.

William was now heir to Penrose and its estates but, not wishing to live in a place associated with such sad events, gave them to another branch of the family, took up his pilgrim's staff again, and left for the Holy Land. There he died, years later. The orchard where his nephew was buried has almost disappeared but a solitary tree is said to mark the grave, in a meadow near to the manor.

... POWERFUL MAGIC ...

Dyonysius Williams lived at Mayon, where he had a reputation as an insightful astrologer and experienced magician. It was his habit each year to collect huge quantities of furze and build it into a rick but was puzzled when it seemed to disappear faster than he could possibly burn in his own house. So he consulted his books and discovered that a number of women from

Sennen Cove had been taking it on a regular basis. The very next night, at a time when all honest folks should be fast alseep, he waited. It wasn't long before an old woman arrived, made a bundle of furze from the rick and tied it with a rope - but when she tried to lift it onto her back, could not move it. She took out half the bundle and put it back, but still couldn't lift it. Now she became frightened and tried to take her rope and run, but she hadn't the strength to do either. The magician had put a spell on her, and there she stayed throughout that cold winter's night. It was not until the next morning that Dyonysius Williams released her. As she was a poor old soul he took pity on her and let her have a 'burn' of furze - but she never came again, nor did any of the other women.

... AND KING ARTHUR.

One of the stronger traditions of King Arthur in this region is that of the battle of Vellan-Druchar. Following several unopposed raids, 'Sea Kings' or 'Danes' landed at Gwenvar, near Sennen Cove, prompting Merlin to make one of his melancholy predictions:

> The Northmen wild once more will land; And bleach their bones on Escall's sand; The soil of Vellan-Druchar's plain; Again will take a sanguine stain; And o'er the millwheel roll a flood; Of Danish mixed with Cornish blood; When thus the vanquished find no tomb; Expect the dreadful day of doom.

This time they arrived in large numbers, intent on penetrating deep inland. They crossed the peninsula, destroying as they went, but a chain of warning beacons had been lit sending the alarm quickly through the length of Cornwall. As the invading army made their way back to their ships they were met by Arthur who with nine kings had marched from Tintagel or Celliwic. The two forces met at Vellan-Druchar, a mile east of St Buryan. The battle was so fierce that the nearby millwheel was powered by blood. Just where that mill was is uncertain for though Kemyel Mill stood two miles away it was worked by a different stream. The result was a crushing victory for Arthur, whose men pursued the surviving invaders westwards to their ships. However during their absence a wise woman had raised a westerly gale by emptying the holy well and sweeping the church, possibly the destroyed Chapel Idne at Sennen Cove, from door to altar. The gale and the tide drove the ships up the beach, stranding the remaining invaders, who were killed, while their ships rotted where they lay. Arthur worshipped at the holy well and later held a victory feast on Table-Maen.

LAND'S END

THE LOST LAND OF LYONESSE

Land's End. A simple name yet encompassing an undeniable grandeur, where mighty Atlantic waves, born a thousand miles away around Nova Scotia, pound relentlessly against soaring, jagged granite cliffs sending great swathes of spray into the air. Not for nothing did our ancestors call it the 'Sea of Storms'. Stand here and you are looking over the lost land of Lyonesse. From this rocky terrain it becomes a reality.

Lyonesse was a prosperous land stretching from the mainland to the Isles of Scilly. It was inhabited by a noble race of people who worked its rich, fertile pastures, building five busy beautiful cities with a total of 140 splendid churches. But this earthly paradise was not to last.

Whether some dreadful sin caused divine retribution is unknown but in one cataclysmic night the whole of Lyonesse disappeared. A tremendous storm blew up, the sea rose ever higher and a vast rush of waves caught the sleeping people unawares, engulfing the cities and churches in rapid succession. Since then it has lain below the stretch of sea which separates the newly-created cliffs of Land's End and the just-born Scilly Isles.

Only one person survived, one solitary man riding a white horse which galloped so fast that it was able to keep in front of the tidal wave. Legends vary as to who this was and three great Cornish families claim descent from him: a Trevelyan or a Trevilian who escaped on this legendary horse carrying him safely to reach ground at Perranuthnoe on Mount's Bay seconds before he was overwhelmed by the wall of water; a Vyvyan whose descendants settled at St Buryan but later moved to Trelowarren near Helston, and who was carried to safety by a white horse; or a Lord of Goonhilly who founded Chapel Idne at Sennen Cove in thanks for his deliverance. All have their modern supporters. The Trevelyan coat of arms still features a white horse outpacing the waves, a perpetual reminder of the one which carried their ancestor. The Vyvyans have as their family crest a white horse, saddled but riderless, while the family is said to have kept a similar one in their stables, saddled ready for any future crisis which fortunately has never come.

Though Lyonesse now lies beneath 28 miles of treacherous seas, for local fishermen the lost land is very much a reality. Its capital, the City of Lyons, is said to have been built around the former hill which is now the dangerous Seven Stones reef. Seamen from the distant past claimed to have trawled up evidence of former buildings, with tools, pots, windows, doors and other household chattels entangled in their nets. Even now they call the area between the Stones 'Trigva', dwelling. More mysteriously they tell you that on a quiet day when the sea is calm you can hear the ghostly bells of churches gently tolling under the rocking waves, and on clear days or moonlit nights if you look down through the water you will see the remains of a great cathedral and many other fine buildings.

Is there any evidence to support the legend? Well, we have a date for the cataclysm, the Saxon Chronicle stating that "... *the Lioness was destroyed on November 11, 1099.*" Later writers accepted Lyonesse as an established fact. As late as 1602 Richard Carew declared

> *The encroaching sea hath ravined from it the whole country of Lyonesse, together with divers other parcels of no little circuit, and that such a Lyonesse there was, these proofs are yet remaining.*

So what is the truth of the compelling tale of the land which sank beneath the sea? There is little doubt that such a submergence did occur, particularly around Mount's Bay, Land's End and the Isles of Scilly, though the chronology which the folklore hints at is wrong. It occurred many, many thousands of years ago. Moreover, the rising sea level was a gradual process over a period of centuries, not a sudden tidal surge. So is it possible that the origin of Lyonesse stems from an ancient, archetypal memory of a real event, condensed in time? And did the ancestor of the Trevelyans or Vyvyans or Lords of Goonhilly note the sea making gradual inroads and then move his family inland before danger struck?

There is also room in Lyonesse for King Arthur. One tradition claims that the treacherous Mordred actually survived the battle of Camlann and pursued the remnants of Arthur's army along the spine of Cornwall where they hoped to gain refuge in what is now the Scilly Isles. Unnoticed though, a strange cloud had travelled ahead of the traitor's forces. As they arrived in the middle of Lyonesse it transformed into the ghost of Merlin who uttered a terrible spell. Immediately a violent storm swallowed them and plunged the doomed land together with Mordred and his soldiers beneath several fathoms of water - where they have remained ever since. Arthur's men were now safe on the hilltops which from that moment had become the Isles of Scilly and later founded a religious house on Tresco in thanks for their deliverance.

Clearly much of the lore of Lyonesse can be dismissed as just too fantastic. But as you stand on the great corrugated cliffs at Land's End, some dropping sheer to the sea, some stacked together and descending in tiers, the Lost Land seems very close. Now imagine the roofscape of towers and spires and ringing church bells which so many people claim to have seen and heard - and who needs further proof? Let Lyonesse retain its secrets.

NANJIZAL COVE

A DROWNING MAN RETURNS ...

In the declining light of a January afternoon a party was in full swing in the best room, the 'parlour', of a farmhouse at Nanjizal Cove. The guests were from local families who had been established here for generations, and some ten to a dozen of their daughters had their eye on the host's eldest son, Joseph, then about twenty years of age.

The farmer and his wife had been persuaded by their two daughters, Mary and Honour, to hold a 'tea and heavy cake party' so that Joseph could be on display. And here they were, involved in all the local gossip and talking about how a ship had been wrecked off Land's End a few

PORTHGWARRA BEACH

ST MICHAEL'S MOUNT

MERRY MAIDENS

ST LEVAN'S STONE

BOTALLACK MINE

PENGERSICK CASTLE

days earlier from which large quantities of fruit were now washing into Nanjizal Cove. Their excitement increased when, gallant as ever, Joseph said he would take one of the farmworkers and get some oranges for the ladies.

As the setting sun illuminated the room in which the party had assembled, outside darkness was fast approaching. The girls continued with their chattering, but Joseph's mother became anxious about her favourite son: why was he taking so long? Mary, Honour and the others tried to ease her mind: there were many fruit-gatherers in the Cove and Joseph was having to search hard for the promised oranges. His mother's anxiety deepened, but after what seemed an age she saw him returning. Relieved, she left the room to let him into the house.

She expected to meet Joseph at the farmhouse door. He was not there. He must have got wet in the Cove and gone round to the kitchen door, to dry himself or to change his boots. She herself went to the dairy to collect the basin of clotted cream. Strangely, all the pans of milk were agitated, "*the milk rising up and down like the waves of the sea,*" she later related. She returned to the parlour, now feeling very uneasy. No-one had seen Joseph. He had not been into the room. She sank heavily into a chair.

Neither Joseph nor the worker returned alive. They had been standing on a rock, bending down to gather oranges brought in on each wave, when they were engulfed by a heavy swell and swept off. Though both men were powerful swimmers the undertow of the current was so strong that they were quickly beyond reach.

The house of partying became a house of mourning. It was nine days before the bodies were recovered, badly mutilated. Over many long years the mother spoke of how she had seen Joseph, there could be no mistake, he was clear and distinct as he passed the parlour window, looking in at her and smiling.

... AND A PHANTOM PEKINESE DOG BITES

As you walk over Nanjizal Cove, look out for a Pekinese dog. If you see it, keep your distance, as its bite brings certain, extremely painful death.

There was a time when only the Imperial family of China were allowed to own Pekinese dogs, but in 1559 the Emperor sent a breeding pair as a coronation gift to Elizabeth I from one royal person to another. His daughter, the Imperial princess, was given the job of ensuring their safety and making the presentation.

It was a long journey. The Pekinese bitch travelled in a carved ivory chest but the dog ran about freely. Three months into their travels five pups were born, which snuggled with their mother in the ivory box while the male stood guard. The party reached France and a Cornish ship was chartered to carry them to London. But the crew had never seen a Chinese lady before: her features, her language, her manners, her dress, marked her out as something very different. She must be a demon, and, moreover, the ivory box over which she took such great care must contain priceless treasure!

As they approached Land's End the ship ran into an unexpected storm. The foreign 'demon' was blamed and she was thrown overboard. The box and its contents were being heaved over the rails when the dog, still trying to protect the bitch and pups, bit one of the crew on his hand. His reaction was automatic, picking it up and throwing it as far into the sea as he could. By daybreak the storm had subsided and the ship was able to enter Mount's Bay. On the same tide the body of the Chinese princess and her ivory chest were washed ashore in Nanjizal Cove.

A local farmer found them. The dog was just about alive. It watched as the man buried all the bodies in the sand and laid a bunch of wild daisies over them. Gently, the man placed the dog amongst the flowers and as gently it licked his hand as it died.

The Cornish ship reached Newlyn but within a few days the bitten sailor died in excruciating agony. Since then other people have been bitten by a Pekinese dog when they have been digging the sand here at Nanjizal, and all have died in considerable pain. Only a couple of hundred years ago a young man found a piece of carved ivory at the bottom of the cliffs, and it bit him - he died within days from what appeared to be merely a superficial wound.

So as you walk the narrow paths and enjoy the truly picturesque beauty of the Cove, watch out for dogs, especially a Pekinese dog - and beware of digging in the sand in case you too come across a piece of ivory!

WALK DIRECTIONS

Distance 5½ miles (8.75km)		Time 3 hours	
Map OS Landranger 203 349263		Terrain	Usually good walking all year round, with modest slopes from sea level up to 300 feet, and one steep one.
Car Parking	Park at Sennen harbour		

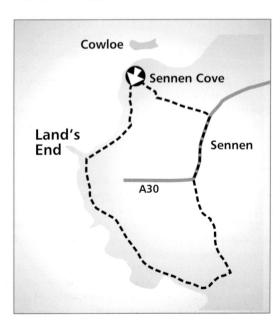

>> From the harbour take the Coast Path, signed to 'Mayon Cliff', going up the concrete steps and heading for the castellated watch tower on the top of Pedn-men-Du. From here there are views of Land's End and the Longships light. *Below you is the statuesque Irish Lady, a detached block of rock perched precariously on top of a pinnacle. Many years ago a ship sailing from Ireland was driven onto these rocks in a ferocious storm. Everyone on board was drowned except for one young lady who was washed onto the pinnacle, to which she clung desperately before resolutely pulling herself up its face. Here she remained for several days, hanging on for dear life, unable to move upwards and trapped by the boiling waves below. Day by day the chances of survival receded until she was overcome by the cruel winds and intense cold, thirst and sheer exhaustion, and she fell onto the rocks below. The tragedy is that in the storms and lashing rain no-one had known until her pathetic body, wearing only a thin white dress, was discovered mangled and limp at the base of the cold granite cliffs. On stormy nights she can be seen, still wearing that white dress, clinging to the rock.* This cliff extends from Sennen to Land's End, so stay on the Coast Path until where the path forks you bear left to reach the hotel.

>> Make for the white painted Greeb Cottage, which is the HQ of a small wildlife park. Go behind the animal enclosures and follow the signpost onto the Coast Path.

>> Continue around Pordenack Point with its spectacular rocks and pinnacles, beyond which is the craggy headland of Carn Boel, while ahead you will see a white house which overlooks Nanjizal Cove. *At Nanjizal, the sands are formed of pure white shells, and there is a natural archway leading to a pool-filled grotto known as 'The Song Of The Sea'.*

>> At the waymark post at Bosistow Cliff turn sharp left and climb the path through the rocks and gorse up the side of a valley. Walk along this path on the top, keeping the white house on the opposite side of the valley. A few yards before the end of the path you pass another marker post, where you keep straight on before going through the kissing gate on your left.

>> Cross the field diagonally left to the corner, as if heading towards the tower of Sennen church. In the next field make for the top left hedge, and keep this hedge on your left until you come to the farm.

>> Keep straight on past the farmyard, cross over the stone stile and pass through the third farmyard to reach stone steps by a gate on the far side, with the farmhouse on your left. Follow the right edge of a field, passing an ancient granite cross, go up the steps and through the gate at the end of the field heading towards a cottage. Go through the cottage's garden and emerge onto the road.

>> Go straight on and join the main road close to the Wreckers Pub. Here, turn right and go past the 'First and Last' pub. *The 'First and Last' is haunted by the ghost of Annie Treeve, who owned the pub in the early part of the nineteenth century. She also ran the local smuggling operation before Customs officers caught up with her. To save her skin Annie turned King's Evidence and for this her neighbours extracted revenge. She was staked out on Sennen beach and left to drown in the incoming tide. Her body was then taken back to the inn before being buried in an unmarked grave. Not surprisingly her ghost is extremely restless - either because she is seeking vengeance or is unable to accept that her smuggling days are long since past.*

>> Walk past Sennen church. When you arrive opposite the shop (but before the petrol station) turn left down the footpath to Sennen harbour and your car.

PORTHGWARRA

DESPERATE LOVERS ...

Just below Tol-Pedn-Penwith is a tiny cove. Years ago folk here lived by fishing and smuggling. For fishermen it was dangerous, negotiating the narrow rows of razor-sharp rocks guarding its long sandy channel before winching their boats up the steep beach. For smugglers it was perfect, connected to surrounding villages only by tiny lanes winding over the granite landscape, and in the eighteenth and nineteenth centuries was the haunt of *soi-disant* 'gentleman' who brought in contraband brandy from France, using their social standing as a cover for their illegal activities. It was not only men who were involved in this risky, if lucrative, business. The ballad *The Female Smuggler* relates the story of Martha Blewett who specialised in smuggling salt before she was murdered near here in 1792.

It was also the scene of a tragic romance. Do you know that the hamlet was once called 'Sweetheart's Cove'? And that on the cliffs at Hella Point is a patch of land known as 'Nancy's Garden'?

Nancy was the only daughter of a rich farmer whose land stretched from their home at Roskestal right down to the sea three-quarters of a mile away. They employed a young man, William, as a farm 'servant', and although he was only an ordinary fisherman's son, Nancy and he fell in love. It was common in those days for men to go to sea during the summer, returning to the farm when winter storms were at their worst. This arrangement suited Nancy's parents as they disapproved of the relationship. Her father in particular considered William an unworthy suitor and tried to prevent the couple from seeing each other, but as lovers do they continued to meet in secret, at night, and pledge their everlasting faithfulness. In the end Nancy's father offered a compromise. First, William must go to sea for three years to make his fortune. If after such a time the young couple still felt the same about each other he would consent to their marriage. Even then the pair contrived a brief meeting. In Porthgwarra Cove under the light of a full moon, Nancy swore that she would never marry another man; William vowed that he would be true to her and, no matter what, would return one day to claim her as his bride.

Next day William joined his ship. Nancy waited. Three years passed. Every-one thought William had forgotten her but Nancy kept her promise and refused to meet any other young men. Day after day she walked to Hella Point from where - at a place on the cliffs which local people later renamed 'Nancy's Garden' - she searched out to sea for sight of the sails of William's ship. In vain. Gradually her sadness became overwhelming. William's continued absence was unbearable. She withdrew from normal communication with people, refused to eat or speak, and spent her days just rocking to and fro, looking for the ship that never came.

Until, that is, one night she heard William tapping at her window, urging her to come to him at the cove where his boat was waiting. What a transformation! Nancy dressed and hurried to Porthgwarra Cove. Actually, all this had been seen by Nancy's old aunt Prudence, who followed and watched from the cliff-top. As Nancy got near the water's edge a young man appeared suddenly at her side, his face deathly pale, his clothes dripping wet. Together they seemed to float over the rocks before stepping into the breakers towards a small boat moored at the entrance to the sandy channel. Briefly a dense, swirling mist veiled them from Prudence's sight and by the time it cleared boat and lovers had disappeared.

Neither Nancy nor William were seen again - but news came to Porthgwarra that half way across the world William's ship had foundered and he had drowned that very same day.

RAFTA

MADGY FIGGY

Madgy Figgy came from Rafta. As leader of the fearsome band of St Levan witches, she was one of the most notorious ever to fly over Cornwall. Her coven met at various places around here, particularly at Tol-Pedn where she could be seen leaping from top to top of the jagged rocks or from where she would lead her followers as they flew on their ragwort stems to Castle Peak, a tall pinnacle at Treryn Dinas, or to the Witch's Rock at Zennor.

Around here village folk were frightened of Madgy Figgy. No-one could counteract her withering spells and in return for her protection gave her everything she asked - including help in wrecking. It was not necessary for them to lure ships onto the rocks by shining false decoy lights. Madgy Figgy took care of that. Here on her giant cuboid rock in the great pinnacle of the Cliff Ladder, still called the Witch's Chair, she would sit with her cauldron and potions scouring the horizon and when a ship was sighted cast spells to summon ferocious storms, gloating and rubbing her hands as it was driven towards land. As the doomed ship foundered on the rocks below, the cliffs echoed the croaking, malicious delight of the malevolent crone. Madgy rejoiced as every desperate man, woman and child drowned, providing her coven with rich pickings. She then hovered above the carnage and plunder, choosing whatever she wanted for herself as her wreckers awaited their prize.

On one occasion Madgy lured a Portuguese Indiaman into Perloe Cove. As the bodies of the crew and passengers were washed ashore her band of witches fell on them, searching and stripping them of every valuable item. This was a rich haul. There had been many wealthy people aboard. Madgy selected one of the corpses as her share of the pickings, that of a young and beautiful woman decked out in gold jewellery, opals, topaz, rings of sapphires and rubies, and loveliest of all a necklace of lozenge-shaped emeralds each within a cluster of tiny diamonds. As Madgy examined the body she noticed a mark on it. Straight away she understood its significance. As always an argument developed between Madgy, her witches and the local wrecking crew who had come to the scene for whatever spoils they could get, sharing them according to a formula she alone determined. Only then was the jewellery belonging to the drowned young woman heaped in a chest in Madgy's hut.

That same night the corpse was buried on the cliff-top but before morning a strange blue light appeared in the cove, rising from the grave and settling on Madgy's own chair on Tol-Pedn. Here it remained for a short time before moving on to Madgy's hut where it sat on the chest. This happened for three consecutive nights - then stopped. A few days later a stranger, clearly foreign, arrived at the cottage and demanded to be taken to the graves of those washed up from the recent wreck. Without hesitating he went straight to the grave of the rich lady, then sat by it through the day. When night fell the weird light rose from it again, shining even brighter, and again made its way to Madgy's hut where it settled on the chest. Hurrying, the stranger followed. As he opened the chest Madgy, recognising that his power was greater than her own, handed all the priceless jewels to him - on which he disappeared. Madgy told everyone that the lady too had been a witch and that only she had known the significance of the mark on the body. She had protected them. If they had destroyed the lady's treasure they themselves would have been destroyed. Now the Tol-Pedn Coastwatch Station counters Madgy Figgy's powers.

ST LEVAN

A SAINT'S PROHECY

St Levan's little church is sheltered away from the village, on a site chosen to retain panoramic views of the sea. Originally though it was to be built at Rafta, at the head of the valley, but as the stones were laid by the workmen they were spirited away every night to where the church now stands - so it was decided to let it rest here.

Levan lived on a diet of one fresh fish a day, which he caught himself - no wonder he is the patron saint of anglers! Despite his piety though he refused to fast on the Sabbath, considering his monotonous diet sufficient penance. Nor did he suffer fools lightly. As he set out one Sunday on his daily fishing trip, a local woman named Johanna, tending her garden and gathering herbs and vegetables for her devoutly meatless dinner, self-righteously rebuked him for his behaviour on a Sabbath. His reply was equally forthright: fishing was no worse than gardening! By now quite incensed, Levan continued to shout in unsaintly manner that any future child born in the parish and christened Johanna would grow up to be as big a fool as she. Since then none have but a piece of ground nearby is still called 'Johanna's Garden'.

Inside the church you can see a bench-end portraying two fish on one hook. The craftsman who carved this unusual subject was well aware of folklore about Levan. One evening about sunset he was fishing as usual from his rocks when there was a heavy pull on his line. He had caught two chad or bream on the same hook. Needing only one he threw them both back, but miraculously again and again they returned to the hook, insisting on being caught together. In the end, convinced there was some reason for this that he couldn't grasp, he took them home to Bodellen and gave them to his sister St Breage, who served them to her two hungry children. This seemingly kindly act contained the seeds of disaster. Eating ravenously the children didn't take out the bones and both choked to death. Since that day chad or bream has been known over a fairly wide area as 'chuck-cheel', choke-child.

Between his fishing trips St Levan used to relax on a massive, rounded boulder just outside the church porch, and almost certainly a pre-Christian sacred rock. One day when he was an old man his temper again got the better of him and he struck the stone with his fist, splitting it through. Praying over it he prophesied in an odd verse:

When with panniers astride,
A pack-horse one can ride
Through St Levan's Stone
The world will be done.

The boulder is still split in two, though happily the gap is only fourteen to twenty inches wide - too narrow for a pack-horse, with or without panniers. Nor has it increased noticeably for centuries. So there is no need to worry about doom and destruction just yet. Don't take our word for it, check for yourselves.

A grim legend cloaks another part of the churchyard. On 18 December 1811, the Scillonian brig *Aurora* was wrecked on the Runnell Stone. The crew escaped in a rowing boat but the master, Captain Richard Wetherall, himself from the Scillies, refused to leave his ship. As he went down he gave orders for one last desperate ring of eight bells. Days later his body was washed up in the cove below and buried here. Now those same ghostly bells can be heard tolling from his grave, indicating to anyone who hears them that their own life's 'watch' is over and they are destined to die within twelve months.

PORTHCURNO

THE PHANTOM SHIP

Cornwall's rugged coastline has long governed the lives of its inhabitants, so it is hardly surprising that people who believed in spirits on land should also find them at sea. Phantom ships have long been tokens of ill-omen, warnings of approaching storms or shipwrecks. There is one at Porthcurno. When evening mists are rising, a ghostly black square-rigged sailing ship comes in from the sea. Many people have seen it - all have regretted it.

A mile inland is Chegwidden Farm, which in the eighteenth century - then called Chygwiden - was occupied by a cantankerous old man and his young second wife. The eldest son by the first marriage, Martin, was treated particularly harshly, leaving him in no doubt about his future here. So Martin ran off to sea and after several years in which he failed to return was presumed dead. The property then passed to a young relative and his teenage sister, Eleanor.

Several years later still Martin returned. Accompanied by a dark-skinned servant and several heavy chests he was dropped off at Porthcurno by a passing ship. Although he could now claim Chegwidden he had no intention of asking his young relatives to leave. For the most part Martin and his foreign companion, Jose, kept themselves to themselves though there was no doubt how they spent their time: they drank heavily, they maintained a form of wild hunting through the night with an unseen pack of hounds whose cries disturbed the countryside round about, and they spent money like there was no tomorrow. Over the months Martin built a half-decked boat which he kept at Porthcurno. Every day he and Jose would put to sea, even during the roughest storms, rarely returning until it was night, often staying out until the next day and occasionally being away for weeks on end. Naturally the locals took an interest and soon the rumour got about that they were pirates. As a consequence most people avoided the strange pair, though Eleanor enjoyed their company and in return was given expensive clothes and jewellery - and people gossiped about that, too.

Martin was much older than the others and made Jose and Eleanor swear that when the time came they would take him out to sea to die and bury him there. Unfortunately Martin's planning went awry and he died sooner than expected. Curiously, as he had never spoken to anyone but Martin, Jose asked a few of the the villagers to carry the coffin to St Levan churchyard but at the same time was seen dragging heavy boxes on board the boat - one of which, local gossip went, contained Martin's body. This appeared to be confirmed when, together with Martin's favourite dog, Jose and Eleanor put to sea. They had gone less than a mile when a tremendous storm blew up. The howling onshore wind lasted for nearly a week and Porthcurno was choked with so much sand that from that day to this it has not been possible to keep a boat of any size in the cove. Martin's was the last.

Stranger still, no sooner had the wind dropped and the lashing rain ceased than a black, spectral boat, identical to Martin's, came from the sea, sailing into Porthcurno Cove - as she has many times since. Usually she is shrouded in the evening mists which steal in off the water, but just occasionally, if you look closely, you can see on her deck the outlines of two men, a woman and a dog. Everyone who has seen her agrees that she glides over the breakers and when she reaches the shore-line continues to head across the sand, her keel skimming smoothly just above ground, pursuing her course steadily as if it were on water. The route the boat takes is always the same: she moves up the valley to Bodellen, where St Levan lived, then steers to Chegwidden, hovers eerily over the farmhouse before bearing away to a cottage and then disappearing near a rock. Don't be surprised if sometime in the future you hear that a large hoard of foreign coins has been found underneath it!

TREEN

THE GIANTS OF TRERYN DINAS ...

According to archaeologists, Treryn Dinas was built on the promontory above Porthcurno by an army of Iron Age workers toiling for many years to construct a fort they could defend from landward by erecting massive outer and inner ramparts with three smaller banks in between across the 310 yards (274m) neck of the headland, and from seaward naturally by the vertical cliffs and jagged rocks. But we know differently. Why otherwise would it be called Giant's Castle? It was conjured up from beneath the sea by a powerful giant who lived here and from where he commanded all the lands west of Penzance. In a hole in a rock, still called Giant's Lock, he put a round stone and declared that if anyone ever removed this 'key' then Treryn Dinas and all its inhabitants would disappear under the sea. And that was before Treryn Dinas became plagued by the spirits of departed witches!

So the earliest inhabitants of this stronghold were giants. Like most of them they had a reciprocal relationship with their human neighbours whom they protected in return for sheep, cattle and other food. There came a time though when one of these giants got to middle age without having children to perpetuate the race. Having no work to do, he grew fat and lazy; as his wife had no housework to take her mind off things she became peevish and petulant. The result was marital strife. Though he was a quiet, good-natured giant she nagged him to rock the Logan Stone for hours rather than just sit and doze in his Giant's Chair - which we can still see. She nagged him to swim out to Dollar Rocks, two miles away, to dive for congers so she could use their fat to make a cake, and catch cod and pollock which they could eat. Sometimes he did as he was told and brought home a string of fish a furlong in length. Often though he just fell asleep. Then his wife would throw rocks at him, heaps of which you can still see lying about just as they dropped near the poor giant's chair. He always woke up to another torrent of abuse.

Not surprisingly, he got fed up with this, but what could he do about it? So one summer's eve he went to Treen and asked the villagers for their advice. That was the opportunity they had been waiting for. They had been very concerned about the absence of giant children to continue their protection, so all sorts of charms and potions were suggested. None worked. Time passed and still the rock-hewn cradle remained empty. Until one villager came up with a solution. Why not steal a baby from the troublesome, aggressive giant of Maen, who had a large family and surely wouldn't miss just one?

To the giant and his wife this was perfect. But who could carry out this baby-stealing without alerting the Maen giant? He was notoriously fierce. A witch was given the job so one afternoon she flew to Cairn-men-ellas and hid between the rocks. Shortly, just before sunset, a giant's child, about four years old, came by. He was not as bright or alert as a human child and had no notion of danger, so the witch had no difficulty in enticing him away with all sorts of promises about the games they could play. When they arrived at Treryn Dinas the giantess greeted them with open arms.

It was just as she had hoped. During his infancy the giant child often sat in a small rock chair which you can still see near the large one where the giant himself rested. In summer the proud old giant would take the child to Castle Peak, stand him on the topmost stone and teach him the names of all the places from Lizard Point to Pedn-Penwith, the sea-lashed headlands, the wild carns inland, all of which he owned and one day the child would inherit. Sometimes they would go to Castle Leas, the giant's favourite fishing place where he had dug out a deep pit to catch fish - and which you can still see. From the rocks at the water's edge the giant put the boy on his back and swam round Sees Rock, where they would eat shags' eggs, limpets and mussels. Then when he was a few years older the giant taught his 'son' to fish from the rocks, how to make hooks from bones and shells - for in the times of giants they hadn't any metal.

The giantess took her responsibilities equally seriously. In fact all her care and attention were lavished on the boy. Her husband was neglected. He had to cook his own fish and to skin his own oxen. He was not allowed to eat sheep as they were reserved for the boy. The giantess began to taunt him again and make comparisons between him and the pampered boy. Worst of all, maternal affection turned to passionate love.

The old giant was slow to see what was happening until he found himself utterly disregarded by both his wife and adopted son. He thought about it as deeply as giants could, reflecting on how they stole away to be together, to be by themselves in sunny spots between the carns, but still avoided any confrontation, until some women from Treen who had spied on the giantess and her son reported the details to him. Now he had no alternative.

From that day he gave them little opportunity to be alone. He wanted to know where they were going and checked where they had been, following them, coming upon them unawares. The time came though when he had to leave the castle to collect provisions from his human neighbours. Even then he gave instructions that one of them should meet him on his return journey to help carry whatever he had got. Both promised.

In this unexpected opportunity to be alone together the pair forgot all about the giant - until they heard his heavy footsteps stamping along Pedn-y-vounder. They had good reason to be afraid, so the giantess climbed on the rocks of the Gap, a dozen feet or so above the narrow path. Her husband came stamping along, an ox on his shoulders, a sheep under each arm, roaring angrily, threatening vengeance as he entered the castle's inner enclosure and found no-one there to meet him. He didn't notice his wife. As he came along the narrow ledge she hit him between his eyes with such a powerful blow that he went head over heels down the precipice, cattle and sheep flying through the air. Though his skull was very thick, it was smashed to pieces on the boulders.

Seeing him falling brought the giantess to her senses. She stepped back twenty paces or so onto a level rock, pulling her apron over her head to blot out the sound of his moaning. He had just enough strength to curse her. Instantly, she was turned to a granite block on the very spot where she stood - and where we can still see the Giant's Lady Rock.

... THE END OF THE PENDARS

For generations the Pendars lived in grand style in their ancestral property at Baranhual, north of Penberth Cove towards St Buryan. Until, that is, one of them acted very unwisely.

This generation of Pendars had a remarkable cow, called Rosy. She gave milk prolifically but even from being quite young had always behaved differently from other cattle. There was no problem with milking her but when she had given a certain amount she would call out gently, kick the bucket over and gallop away. After a while Rosy had a heifer calf but even when it had suckled Rosy still gave her usual supply of milk. Then one Midsummer's night the milkmaid returned late from a trip to Penberth. Rosy was waiting impatiently in the field and gave her usual quantity of milk - then lowed gently. Hundreds of fairies appeared around her. One large group gathered under her udders and held butter-cups to catch milk while others sucked it off clover blossoms. Rosy was ever so pleased with herself, trying to lick those on her neck who were scratching behind her horns or picking ticks from her ears, while others smoothed her coat. In return the fairies brought armsful of herbs for Rosy and her calf.

Straight away the maid ran and told her mistress, giving an accurate description of the little folk, about twelve inches tall, the ladies' dresses all bright and well-cut like gentry, their hair flaxen in long curls, the men smartly turned out. Mrs Pendar made a rapid diagnosis: the cow was bewitched. They must get rid of the sprites. Her husband took a different view: he recalled how old folks said that fairies always brought good luck when left alone. Mrs Pendar took no notice. Next morning off she went to Treen to consult a witch. The advice was unequivocal. As fairies disliked salt, she should sprinkle it over the cow, wash her udder in brine and throw it all over the farm.

Mrs Pendar did just that. In the evening she herself went to milk Rosy, carrying two buckets this time. Rosy let Mrs Pendar get into position - then kicked the bucket to pieces, sent Mrs Pendar sprawling, tossed her over her head and galloped off, bellowing. From that day no-one got a drop of milk from Rosy. For days and nights she roamed about the farm, followed by her calf, both calling all the time. By Christmas they had become skinny, covered in lice and had skin ailments. Worst of all, the other cattle on Baranhual deteriorated, too. Mr Pendar, still not knowing what his wife had done, brought all the white witches he knew of to put a stop to this run of bad fortune, for now everything he owned was involved, including blighted crops. Torches were carried round the fields at night. Blood was drawn from the diseased cattle and burned. Healthy cattle were forced through flames of bonfires. Nothing worked.

More than a year passed and Mr Pendar decided to sell Rosy and her calf at the next St Buryan Fair. All the Baranhual men and boys helped but could get them neither to the Fair nor home again. As they galloped about, Mr Pendar followed them on horseback and caught just a glimpse of Rosy and her calf racing over Sennen Green towards Gwenvar Sands. They were never seen again. Mrs Pendar suffered all sorts of bone and joint ailments. The milkmaid became so dowdy no young man ever fancied her. Everything went wrong with the family and within this generation the Pendars hadn't an acre of land to their name.

So next time you are visited by fairies, don't interrupt them.

WALK DIRECTIONS

Distance   7½ miles   Time   3¾ hours
Map   OS Landranger 203 372217 Terrain Mostly moderate through level fields but
                                              there are some steep coastal sections, from
                                              sea level up to 300   feet (93m), and steps
                                              along the rocky but well-defined path.
Car parking   Porthgwarra.

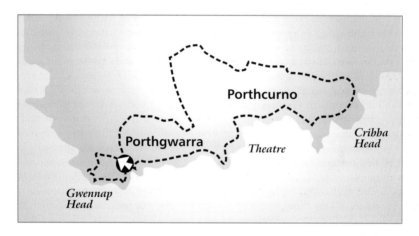

Porthgwarra Cove consists of a little beach flanked by granite cliffs, with several caves and tunnels, some natural and some carved from the rock. These were used by smugglers and by fishermen for storing gear and beaching their boats.

>> Turn right out of the car park and head up the surfaced road to Gwennap Head Coastwatch station. Below is Madgy Figgy's 'Chair Ladder', an enormous pinnacle of granite blocks, a lustre of yellow and green, red and orange enhanced by lichen and the weather, from which she and her cronies summoned sea mists and drew ships onto the treacherous rocks below.

Gwennap Head is known as Tol-Pedn-Penwith which in Cornish means 'the headland with a hole', and indeed there is a collapsed cave on the point..

>> Turn left at the Coastwatch look-out and walk along the cliff-top, branching right just before two coned daymarks, waymarked 'Coast Path', to Hella Point.

Try to imagine the scene three hundred years ago, when this was a very remote spot. Picture a driving winter storm and a beautiful young girl, Nancy, on the grassy precipice, gazing out to sea and pining for her absent lover. Herein lies Cornwall's scenic magic intermixed with fascinating folklore. The jagged rocks below the Point and around Polostoc Zawn remind us how perilous this coastline was in the days of sail and just how difficult William's job was.

As you pass the two brightly-painted concrete cones protruding from the heather, which are landmarks to assist sailors fix the position of the dangerous Runnel Stone Reef, you will probably hear the errie sound of the Runnel Stone Buoy, a mile out to sea. Not for nothing is it known locally as 'Moaning Minnie'.

>> When you reach a metalled road, turn right and continue down into Porthgwarra Cove. Walk around the back of the beach slipway.

>> Go past the cafe/shop and turn right at the signpost. Then go left uphill between the two nearest cottages. Follow the Coast Path acorn signs to your right through the rock tunnel to the top of the cliff, which abounds with wild flowers.

High granite cliffs guard either side of the cove and horses and carts used to be driven down through this tunnel to collect seaweed from the beach for use as fertiliser on the fields above.

>> Continue on the Coast Path. The first cove you descend into rather steeply is Porth Chapel, formerly known as Porth Selevan, another sandy beach hemmed in by sheer granite cliffs.

St Levan's holy well is alongside the Path at the top of the cliff; water from here is still used for baptisms in the church. The remains of the chapel, dating from the eighth century, are on the left of the steps down to the beach.

>> Go across the small wooden bridge bearing left, initially inland, and then to your right downhill at a sign indicating the Coast Path.

>> Continue along the Coast Path, uphill now, until you emerge on the far edge of the spectacular Pedn-men-an-mere headland at the car park for the Minack Theatre.

This was carved out of the rockface to resemble a classical amphi-theatre. You can have a look if there is no performance in progress.

>> Walk straight through the car park to where the track splits into three and take the left one down a steep cliff by rough rock steps onto the beach at Porthcurno. Go across and join the metalled road.

>> Before this road bears round to the right and starts to go uphill, turn off to your left to re-join the Coast Path. This stretch will take you for 2 miles to Treryn Dinas and eventually to Penberth Cove.

>> Before you get there, where the path splits into three, take the right fork which will lead you to the Iron Age cliff castle, thought to have been occupied from the third to the first centuries BC.

This is an area of massive slabs and castle-like blocks of granite, used by the giants who built the fort. Frequent sightings of moving lights and sweet music suggest it is also still home to the Little People.

>> Continue past the castle along the Coast Path, and descend into the tiny but picturesque Penberth Cove. Cross the ancient stone bridge at the head of the harbour over the small stream which runs the length of this valley.

Penberth is an active fishing village, somehow still managing to marry the wild with the picturesque. It was given to the National Trust in the 1950s in memory of those killed in the Second World War.

There is a sad story of how the last of one of the great landowners met his death here. The I'an's had lived at Treen for centuries but one of them, John, was an active smuggler. On one occasion he was returning from Brittany with a cargo of contraband. As his ship approached Penberth the sea was smooth and despite thick fog he ran close in near the Cove. Just at that moment another 'freetrader' was doing the same and in the poor light mistook John I'an's craft for a Revenue cutter. One of the crew fired a shot and I'an was killed outright. The shot was returned and the other vessel was sunk. Almost all the menfolk of Penberth were aboard and the majority drowned within shouting distance of the Cove and their cottages. It also marked the end of the I'an family.

>> Now you will head for Treen. Retrace your footsteps to where there is a large, restored capstan near the coast path.

This was used to pull boats up the huge flat stones which formed a slipway out of the sea before the modern-day winch was installed.

Just after the capstan turn right and follow the footpath, leading up the valley near the small hut. Go through a field gate on the right side of a cottage.

>> The path here is very rocky but is an obvious route as it climbs the hillside, through the gorse and bracken, to where it levels off. Just as you start to go down you arrive at a T-junction. Here turn left onto a path which winds up the hill, curving to your left and then your right through the wood. You emerge from the wood at a field, where you turn right and go round it. Before the gate go through the small gap and over a bank into another field.

>> Cross this field keeping close to the bank on your left. As the field widens, walk diagonally left, climb over the bank and go through the gate, crossing the next field to the standing stone. Here, turn left and go over a stone stile in the bank and into a field. Turn right into a field where cars may be parked. You are now in Treen.

>> Continue across this field diagonally to the car park entrance and onto the metalled lane, passing the chapel on your left. As the lane bends to the right, you turn off left and at the next two forks keep to the right until you go through a gap along the left side of a house. Go over the stile into a field.

>> Walk around the left side of this field and follow the path over the next six stiles and intervening fields to reach a track. At the last turn left down to a field gate at Trendrennen. Turn right, continuing directly up the field to another field gate and into the lower right corner of a field. Now go diagonally left up this field, over the stile, across the right side of another field and emerge onto a lane.

>> Turn right onto the lane for about 100 yards, then turn off left to go over the stone stile onto a footpath. Go across the field to another stile and continue almost directly across another field to another stone stile. Keep to your right, go through the gate in the far right corner and then bear right over the next stile to the gate immediately on the right of Raftra Farm.

This is the hamlet from which Madgy Figgy came. More recently, houses have replaced the ancient huts in which the old witch lived.

>> Go around the left side of the field, past the farm buildings and turn left onto a track near the bottom of the gardens. Where the path forks, take the right hand one, heading towards the hamlet of Rospletha. At Rospletha, at the far end of the houses, go through the kissing gate which is on your left and into a field. This path heads straight towards the tower of St Levan church.

The Celtic cross you pass is one of four placed around St Levan church to ward off pagan influences.

>> Cross several further stiles and fields, which here are relatively small, only three or four acres, and are an indication of early Celtic farming methods. Keep walking in

the same direction until you arrive at a stile on your left half-way down a field.
Cross over and bear right just before a row of cottages to enter the churchyard.
Near the south porch door of the church is the large granite rock, split in two.

>> Leave the churchyard at the top left corner near the granite coffin stile by the
ancient cross and follow the path past the footpath sign in the turning space
opposite the church. Here you enter fields again.

>> Walk up the first field, keeping the boundary to your right, to the stile at the top
and follow the path across a larger field to the remains of another ancient cross. At
the cross turn left, heading towards a stile in the opposite wall. From here take the
walled track down into Roskestal village.

The farm where Nancy lived is just along the lane.

Continue through the village and onto the road. Turn left, and where the road takes
a sharp right turn, walk straight ahead following the footpath waymark. This track
will lead you into Porthgwarra. When you reach a white house on your right, make
a hairpin right turn along its side, and you will come into the Cove and to your car.

Roskestal Farmhouse

BOLEIGH

WITCHES AT TREWOOFE ...

Trewoofe Farm stands at the head of Lamorna Valley. When it was the home of the Lovells, it was much grander but they were one of those families who for generations were unfortunate in their choice of partners. One of them was Squire Lovell. His wife was particularly beautiful, and though he could never catch her at it he suspected she was having an extra-marital *affaire*. One evening, the Squire was out hunting when he startled a large, white hare. Excitedly calling his hounds he gave chase, keeping as close as he could as the hare crossed open country before going to ground in a fogou, one of those curious, man-made, subterranean caves found in Cornwall. Undaunted Lovell leapt from his horse and ran into the dark passage which, as fogous are said to do, went on underground for a considerable distance (though in actuality few are longer than 25 yards). Still he followed - and stopped in a cold sweat. Before his eyes the hare changed into his wife. She went to meet other women at what was clearly a witches' coven assembled round a fire and presided over by a black-clad demon with a forked tail - whom the Squire recognised as her putative lover.

Unable to prevent himself, the Squire swore loudly. As one, the gathering turned, cursing, and attacked him. He tried to defend himself but was so deeply shocked that by the time he got out of the fogou, followed by his hounds now baying wildly in terror and foaming at the mouth, he was quite raving mad. But he did not disappear altogether. His unsettled spirit continues to haunt the fogou and on stormy nights he and his spectral hounds can be seen galloping over the open moorland at nearby Boleigh.

... AND MERRY MAIDENS

Boleigh, scene of the poor, mad Squire's ghostly ride, is the site of a stone circle, one of many of Cornwall's prehistoric monuments which have had fanciful names imposed on them by later Christian societies in reaction to their perceived 'pagan' significance. But folklore tells us that these stones are a perpetual and salutory reminder of Divine displeasure.

For a long time in Cornwall singing or dancing on the Sabbath was considered a very serious sin. In fact playing any music at all was forbidden. Nonetheless, one Saturday night two young men were on their way home after playing their pipes in an inn near St Buryan. They had had a tiring evening and the road was long, so they sat down for a rest and began to play their music. But it had turned midnight. No sooner had they started than they were turned to stone. For many years the two stood here alone by the roadside but on certain nights when the moon was full they came to life and played on their pipes. A curse fell upon anyone who heard them so the locals avoided the place as much as possible.

One fine night though, by a full moon, a group of high-spirited young girls from Lamorna decided to see for themselves what all the fuss was about and, as young girls do, dared one another to go into the field. The Pipers struck up their music, gently at first but with increasing tempo, so enchanting that the girls couldn't stop themselves and began dancing, slowly initially then faster and faster, whirling round and round the field, forming a frenzied circle. But again Saturday night moved into Sunday morning, and still the Pipers played and still the girls danced. Laughing and chattering, they had forgotten all about the Sunday prohibition. Suddenly, as the music and dancing reached fever pitch there was a mighty crack of thunder and a vivid flash of lightning and the merry maidens were transfixed. As dawn came, a search-party of worried parents found them, just nineteen stones, still and silent, but even now when the moon is full they all come to life to continue their dancing. Ungallantly, the Pipers had taken to their heels and left the girls to their fate as soon as the metamorphosis began - but were caught some distance away and they too remain in stone.

Now they remind us of that Saturday night and Sunday morning. The Merry Maidens is an impressive 78-foot-diameter (26m) circle of 19 regularly-placed blocks of local granite, each standing about 4 feet (1.2m) high, dressed to make their tops level and flat. Although no stone is exceptionally large they are enhanced by their specifically chosen site, a place which may be remote but has great atmosphere. They were obviously set carefully in place but archaeologists are far from unanimous about the intentions of our Bronze Age ancestors as they erected them here sometime in the third or second millennium BC. There is no mark on them to throw light on the matter. Were they amphitheatres for these prehistoric men? Did they play a role in some religious rite? Were they druid temples and used for ritual sacrifice? Whatever, they hold a strange fascination. The Pipers, the northernmost measuring 15 feet (4.6m) and its equally slender companion a mere 13 feet 6 inches (4.1m) tall, and 120 feet apart, can be seen some 450-500 yards to the south-east, while another massive monolith nearby is the Fiddler, who also played that night. These may be aligned to the circle but cannot be seen from it, and there is no proven archaeological connection. It doesn't stop us speculating why many standing stones in Cornwall are in pairs, oriented generally east and west and found in open countryside near other monuments. Were they intended to mark the times of the solstice or equinox, or dates of importance to a pastoral economy, or sacred festivals? Is this why early Christians tried to obliterate the folk-memory of their veneration?

There is one historical possibility which is almost as romantic as the folklore. The name Boleigh means 'field of slaughter' and here was the site of the last great battle in the west when the English Saxons led by King Athelstan defeated King Howel and the Celtic Cornish army in AD 935. To celebrate his victory Athelstan gave a charter to found a collegiate church at St Buryan, but were the two immense Pipers erected by the king as peace stones to seal the treaty? Or, as the whole area is marked with barrows and Bronze Age bones, did the Pipers represent rival kings surrounded by the bodies of those killed in battle?

This isn't all. It is said the circle's stones cannot be moved and that attempts to do so have failed. One farmer managed to remove two or three but they found their way back into place by morning. Moreover, the oxen which dragged the stones from their sockets fell down dead.

... WHILE BETTY'S WITCHCRAFT IS PROFITABLE ...

In her younger years, Betty Trenoweth worked as a maid servant to Squire Cardew at his old mansion at Boskenna. It was here she learned from his ageing mother the therapeutic secrets of the wild plants which grew in the fields and lanes. Later, when the Boskenna estate had to be sold and Betty went to live in a small cottage near St Buryan, she began to ramble over the moors and cliffs gathering herbs when the moon was full and making them into ointments and creams to cure all sorts of ailments and conditions. It wasn't long before these were in great demand, especially for skin diseases and allergies. Then Betty Trenoweth became known as a witch. It may have been just gossip at first but other people believed it.

One of them was Dick Angwin. He had fallen out with Betty over some insignificant matter but when his cows went off their legs and other things went wrong around his farm he blamed it on her and decided to punish her by making her image in clay and pushing a long skewer through its body. At that precise moment, Betty fell to the ground, rolling about and groaning in agony. She told those watching to go straight to Dick Angwin's, "*and tell am I'll make et up weth am ef he will.*" Fearing the witch might die and leave her promise unfulfilled, Dick did indeed make friends and destroy the model.

This didn't stop Betty. One market day at the end of harvest she went to Penzance to buy a pig which she could fatten for winter. She saw what she wanted and was negotiating the price when her cousin, Tom Trenoweth, offered more. Betty was furious but Tom refused to back down and Betty went off mumbling threats and curses and shaking her bony finger at him.

Tom led the pig home, put it in a sty, filled the trough with food and fastened the door firmly. But next morning the door was open, the trough still full - and the sow was rooting in a neighbour's garden. It took the men and boys of St Buryan several hours to get the creature back into it's sty, but every night it got out. Sometimes it was found several miles away, having left a trail of damage which Tom had to pay for.

Several months went by and still the sow got out and wandered off - and to Tom's chagrin the more it ate the leaner it became. Until one day Betty met her cousin and asked, as she had heard the pig was causing him considerable trouble, if he was prepared to sell it. Tom wouldn't consider it. Nothing would induce him to sell it to her. Over the next few months Betty made several more offers, each time reducing her price as the pig was getting thinner and would soon be nothing but skin and bone. The time came when Tom had had enough: the pig had cost him more than it was worth and was still getting thinner. So he fastened a rope round one of its legs and set off to Penzance's Thursday market, determined to sell it for whatever he was offered. The sow walked quietly and peacefully enough alongside him until they reached a ford, but here refused to go into the water. Tom could neither push nor pull it across. He tried to hold up its hind quarters and walk it like a wheelbarrow - but it bolted between his legs and ran off over the moor. Tom followed through the bogs and furze for several miles until they reached Leah Lane on the Penzance-to-Land's End road. The sow looked none the worse but Tom was exhausted and his clothes were torn to shreds.

When they got to Tregonebris Downs Tom was able to catch the rope and tie it round his wrist. He would get it to market whatever happened! No sooner had he muttered these words than a hare leapt out of a bush, made a sound and ran over the moor, followed by the sow dragging Tom along until they got to Tregonebris bridge. Here it dashed under the road as far as it could. The opening was too small for Tom to crawl in, his arm was almost pulled out of its socket, the rope was cutting into his skin, so he let go - and the sow went into the middle where the hole was at its narrowest and sat in the water.

Tom could neither drive nor coax his pig out. It just sat and grunted. Hours later, who should come along but old Betty, seemingly surprised to see Tom sitting at the roadside. Again she offered to buy the sow - he was after all her cousin - and this time Tom couldn't agree quickly enough. The old woman went down to the mouth of the bridge and made a sound exactly like the hare had done. Out came the sow and followed her home just like a dog.

Tom walked to Sancras and drank all his money. Every-one who listened to him agreed that the hare was none other than old Betty. She however kept her pig for many years. Under her care it thrived and she successfully reared all its many piglets at a handsome profit.

ALSIA MILL

... BUT NANCY IS NOT AS FORTUNATE

A farmer named Lenine lived in Boscean, helped by his son Frank and one servant, Nancy Trenoweth. Though Nancy was uneducated, and had never been more than a few miles beyond Land's End, she was treated well, more as a daughter than just an employee.

Frank and Nancy came into contact quite a lot and, as young people do, fell in love. Although this was obvious to the neighbours, Frank's parents were appalled when he asked for their agreement to his marrying Nancy: the Trenoweths were much lower class than the Lenines. Nancy was sent back to her parents at Alsia Mill and Frank was ordered never to see her again. What a situation. The Lenines hardly spoke and there were angry arguments between the three of them.

Nonetheless Nancy and Frank spent almost every evening together. Their favourite meeting place was at the holy well and here they exchanged locks of hair and promises of fidelity. One night they even climbed to the Logan Rock at Treryn Dinas and repeated their promises. Then the consquence of spending so much time in the moonlight together became apparent. Nancy's parents discovered she was pregnant. Now Frank would have to marry their daughter. Still Farmer Lenine would not give his consent. Indeed he decided to remove his son from the scene altogether - anything to get over this 'love-madness', as he called it.

Under the continuous onslaught from his parents Frank's resolve weakened. His father took him to Plymouth and enlisted him on a ship bound for India.

A baby was born. From then on all Nancy's time and energy were devoted to its care, until the Trenoweth's hit even leaner times. Nancy had to go into service again, this time in Paul.

Three years passed and no-one had heard of Frank. Next All Hallows Eve, two of Nancy's friends persuaded her to follow the custom of sowing hemp seed with them. At midnight they stole unnoticed into Paul. Nancy was the first to scatter the seed, quoting the incantation

> *Hemp-seed I sow thee, hemp-seed I grow thee,*
> *And he who will my true love be*
> *Come after me and show thee.*

She repeated the words the requisite three times but as she was getting up, over her shoulder she saw an angry Farmer Lenine. She shrieked - and broke the spell. One of the other girls carried on with the ritual, and had a vision of a white coffin. None of them slept that night.

November brought its storms and during one horrendous night a large ship was dashed to pieces on the rocks below Bernowhall Cliff. One of the few washed onto the shore was Frank Lenine, barely alive. His friends carried him on a stretcher to Boscean, but he died as they reached the outskirts. So crushed were his parents with their grief and guilt that they told no-one, not even Nancy. Not even when Frank was buried in St Buryan churchyard.

On the night of the funeral Nancy was going about her normal chores, locking the doors and checking outside, when a horseman rode up with great speed and called her name. She froze. It was Frank Lenine: that she could never mistake. Even in the dim light he looked saddened and very pale, as he told Nancy he had just arrived home and without waiting had got his horse so they could marry straight away. Nancy was so excited. She jumped up behind him, but as she took Frank's hand a cold shiver passed through her. She put her arm round his waist - and it became as stiff as ice. She was deeply afraid, but couldn't make out why. As they dashed into the ford at Trove Bottom Nancy caught sight of the rider's moonlit reflection in the water: he was in a shroud. Nancy knew she was being carried away by a spirit but could do nothing about it.

The horse galloped on and soon they arrived at the blacksmith's forge near St Buryan. Nancy could see the smith was still hard at work. "*Save me, save me, save me,*" she cried as loudly as she could. The smith sprang from the door, a red-hot iron still in his hand, and as the horse rushed by was able to catch Nancy's dress and pull her to the ground. The spirit too seized hold of her dress. The horse continued on, pulling Nancy and the smith along the road as far as the almshouses near the churchyard. There the horse stopped, and the smith was able to burn Nancy's dress out of the rider's hand with the hot iron. Horse and rider leapt over the churchyard wall and vanished on the grave in which Frank Lenine had been laid just a few hours earlier.

Nancy was taken back to Alsia. Before morning, she was dead. That night a horse was seen galloping through St Buryan and in the morning Frank's colt was found dead below Bernowhall Cliff, covered with foam, its eyes protruding from their sockets, its swollen tongue hanging from its mouth. On Frank's grave was the piece of Nancy's dress which had been in the spirit's hand. Poor Nancy was buried in the same grave as her beloved Frank. Within a year the friend who had sown the hemp seed lay beside her.

WALK DIRECTIONS

Distance 6 miles (9.7km)   Time   3½ hours
Map   OS Landranger 203 452242 Terrain Fairly flat along the Coast Path with some
                                             rocky sections. There are several steep
                                             ascents and descents, overall to 558 feet
                                             (170m), and wooded valleys and fields.
Car Parking   Park at Lamorna Cove.

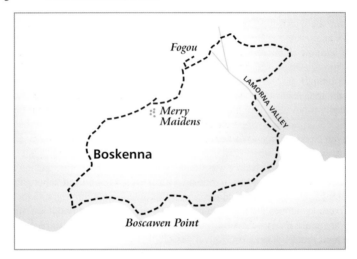

>>   From the jetty above Lamorna harbour take the Coast Path southwest through
      some short rocky sections but still following the acorn waymarks as you pass a
      small Celtic cross on Lamorna Point.
      *This is the 'Silent Cross of Lamorna', about 5 feet tall on a levelled rock, but with
      no inscription, no date - a silent witness to some-one or something. One tradition
      holds that it is a memorial for a little girl called Emma who was drowned with
      eight other children when a ship, the 'Garonne', was wrecked near here in 1868.
      Another that it was put up in memory of a student at Jesus College, Cambridge,
      who in 1873 slipped and fell down the cliffs at this spot and was killed.*
      The cliffs do indeed drop ferociously to your left, so great care is needed. As you
      go over Tregurrow and Rosemodress Cliffs the way becomes less rugged.
>>   There is a stile at the top, then a steep descent before ascending again. On your left
      you pass 'Dorminack', the house and bulb fields made famous by the author Derek
      Tangye, and then the entrance to Tater du Lighthouse, before the Path becomes a
      lane passing on your right a large house, which used to be a row of coastguards'
      cottages, and becomes the Coast Path again.
>>   As you pass Boscawen Cliff, with its logan stone, remember the RNLI crews.
      *It was off Boscawen Point that the whole crew of eight of the Penlee lifeboat
      'Solomon Browne' were drowned while attempting to rescue the crew of the
      'Union Star' that had crashed onto the rocks here in1981.*
      After Boscawen the walking becomes rough again and you begin to descend
      steeply into St Loy's Cove. Cross the large, smoothed boulders and then take the
      path inland by the stream, crossing the small footbridge, and climb up its wooded

valley. Cross the private drive and climb steeply upwards, over the stile to a track and turn right. Cross another stile and follow the path through the trees.

>> At the signpost turn and descend sharply right, crossing the stream before taking the path between the hedges bearing left as you go. In about 50 yards (46m), by another signpost, turn right and walk up to the surfaced lane.

>> Turn left and walk along the lane going uphill. At the junction keep straight ahead, still going uphill. At Boskenna Farm follow the surfaced lane as it bears left and then keep straight ahead.

>> When you reach the bungalow on your right go through the field gate and cross the field to a stile. Go diagonally right across the field to the stile at the top, emerging onto a lay-by with the large granite Boskenna Cross at its edge.

It is difficult to date the cross but it may have been carved just before or during Norman times. Close inspection reveals a carving of Christ, so it is likely to have been a place of worship for those on a journey.

Turn right. It is now necessary to follow the road for about a mile, passing on your right an ancient cross and the 14-feet (3.5m) long Tregiffian Barrow, a Neolithic burial chamber dating from around 4,000 BC.

On the far side is an interesting slab of rock with 25 carvings on it, called 'cup marks'. There are 13 circles and 12 oval shapes. It has been suggested that this has something to do with the full and new moons.

Soon you will arrive at the Merry Maidens, in a field also on your right. Take the footpath sign into the field - and ponder the fate of the young girls.

>> From the stone circle, continue in the same direction to the far left-hand corner of the field and cross the stone stile. Keep diagonally right in this field, and similarly in the next, heading towards the buildings. Go over the stile and you will emerge onto the road. Turn left and walk to the Pipers, on your left, set back a little from the road but access is easy.

You can look back and see the Merry Maidens circle in the field just over the brow of a hill about half a mile away.

>> Continue along the road for another 500 yards (462m), passing the entrance to Boleigh Farm on your left. Take the next lane on your left and go past the house on your right before turning right at the junction with another lane. The Rosemerryn fogou, still haunted by Squire Lovell's tormented spirit, is in the wooded area just behind the property at the end of this lane.

Built during the Iron Age, fogous are as rare and mysterious as they are unexplained. This one is probably the most unusual. Several theories have been proposed about their functions: as a refuge from raiders, as a storage area or as a place of ritual and worship. Rosemerryn gives the strongest evidence for this last. It contains a carving of a human torso and head, the only known Iron Age carving in Cornwall, thought to represent a Celtic god.

>> Retrace your steps to the B3315 and turn left, signed to the ancient hamlet of Trewoofe, where the once-powerful Lovells lived. Where the road bends to the left, you bear right onto a minor made-up public lane. This will lead you down the lovely Lamorna Valley, where you can appreciate the flowers, trees and shrubs, and the way nature has reclaimed the abandoned quarries which in the nineteenth century were worked extensively for their high-quality stone and are now nature reserves. Walk past the Lamorna Wink, to your car.

SANCREED

JENNY AND THE CHANGELING

It is easy to forget how many hazards life held in previous centuries for the people of Cornwall. Spirits, piskeys, fairies, witches, spriggans and knockers must have seemed very close. Spriggans were notorious for stealing human babies, leaving their own mis-shapen offspring in their place. This happened to Jenny Trayer's child.

Jenny lived at the foot of Chapel Carn Brea. Whenever possible she worked as a labourer on nearby farms, doing whatever was available and leaving her baby at home. The hours were long and the work was physically demanding. Almost invariably when she returned home in the evening she was worn out. On this occasion Jenny had been working late in the harvest fields near Penzance and was surprised to find the baby out of its cradle, crawling in a corner of the room amongst the firewood, but Jenny was so weary she just put the child back into its cradle and crawled into her own bed where she slept soundly until morning. Straight away she noticed that the baby had changed. He had always been a contented child, happy to lie gurgling to himself through the day whether Jenny was at home or away at work. Now he gave Jenny no peace: he cried continually, demanding to be breast-fed and attended to. His appearance too had changed: no longer a pink, bonny, plump creature with expressive, saucer-like, blue eyes. Overnight he had become pale, sallow, skinny, wasted, staring.

Poor Jenny Trayer. What a problem she had. There was only one explanation. She suspected straight away - here was a changeling! She told her friends who were also young mothers but they couldn't help, in their anxiety to protect their own babies. They did suggest though that she should consult her older, more experienced neighbours. The latters' advice was to dip it into Chapel Euny Well on the first three Wednesdays in May. Without any hesitation Jenny trudged off to the Well with the squawking, restless brat. On the third Wednesday a gale was blowing but Jenny still made the journey and dipped it into the Well. When they were on their way home both she and the 'baby' heard a shrill voice screeching as if from nowhere
"*Tedrill! Tedrill! Thy wife and child greet thee well!*"
The 'baby's' reaction was immediate and horrifying. Cackling like an old man, it replied that it had no need of any wife or child for it was carried around by its 'mother' and had plenty of milk to feed on. Jenny had been correct. Now she knew the truth. Her 'baby' was a spriggan named Tedrill, an old man who had a wife and child of its own.

Her mood varying between black despair, hysterical disgust and morose self-loathing, Jenny ran home as fast as her legs would carry her - fortunately her 'baby' did not weigh much. She rushed to her neighbours and told them what had happened. Their advice was unanimous and unequivocal. Stronger measures were called for. Now she must put the 'baby' on a pile of ashes and give it a good beating with a broom, then lay it naked under a church stile, leaving it until the next night when, in all probability, the thing would be taken away and her own proper, stolen child returned.

Despite her reluctance to apply such ill-treatment, Jenny did as she was advised. The 'child' roared and roared and Jenny felt terribly guilty - but the remedy produced the result she wanted. Next day under the stile she found her own baby, sleeping soundly in a little nest of straw, beautifully clean and wrapped in a piece of warm, lavender-coloured cloth. Jenny was overjoyed. Never again did she let her baby out of her sight. Without knowing anything of contemporary paediatrics her suspicion had been confirmed. All the same, like every other human child who has been with the fairies this one too was different, singing unknown songs to itself in a strange language and talking to people no-one else could see.

You might find it difficult to believe this tale of Jenny's baby, but changelings were very real to people in Cornwall. As recently as 1843 a Mr J Trevelyan of Penzance was reported in *The West Briton* of 14 July when he was charged with ill-treating one of his children. The boy was frequently starved and kicked by his parents and beaten by the servants, treatment which continued even at Christmas 1841, when still only fifteen months old the child was put into a tree and left in the cold for two-and-a-half hours. Nowadays we might consider this a case of brutal child abuse but to the parents these child rearing practices were quite logical. They believed him to be a changeling, their own child had been stolen by the piskeys - and they wanted him back. When the case came before the magistrates it was dismissed for lack of evidence - but the inhabitants of Penzance took matters into their own hands and drummed the parents out of town. We do not know what happened to the unfortunate boy.

WALK DIRECTIONS

Distance 2¼ miles (3.6km)   Time   1¼ hours
Map   OS Landranger 203 403286 Terrain   Fairly easy across moorland and farmland but with one strenuous climb to 653 feet (198m)
Car parking   Park in the car park west of the hamlet of Brane

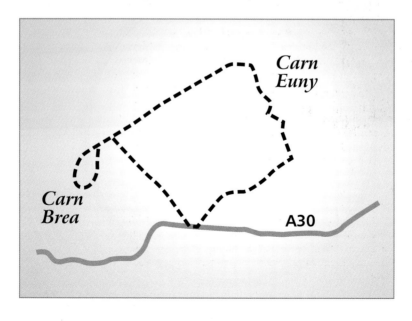

>> From the car park bear left along the lane away from Brane. When you arrive at the junction signed on your right to 'Carn Euny Settlement and Fogou' turn left and then take the first left alongside the stream to Chapel Euny holy well.

This had therapeutic properties which were active only on the first three Wednesdays of each May. It was a wishing well, too. On summer evenings young girls gathered here and threw in pins or pebbles. As these sank near or apart so their future was predicted by the number of bubbles indicating the number of years before they would be united or parted from sweethearts.

>> Return to the path and turn right, crossing Tredinney Common, before emerging onto a minor road. Cross this to the car park. Go through the kissing gate, signed 'Chapel Carn Brea', and turn first right, then first left, ascending to the summit.

From here there are wonderful views in every direction, across the sea and the whole of West Penwith. This spot has long been of religious significance. Two barrows were constructed here during the Bronze Age and millennia later a medieval chapel was built on top, but then destroyed a long time ago.

>> Retrace your steps downhill to the minor road and turn right along it. After about 800 yards (735m), at the junction with the major road, you will pass a Celtic cross.

You don't believe witch's lived around here? Then why is this called Crows-an-Wra, 'witch's cross'? It got this name from a hermit who lived in the chapel on Chapel Carn Brea and was accused by the Dean of St Buryan of being a sorcerer. Then there was the case of fifteen-year-old John Tonken of Penzance, who in April, 1686, began to have fits. A month later, as he lay in bed, he saw an apparition of a strangely-dressed woman who told him he would not be well until he had vomited nut shells, pins and nails. This he did, but a doctor could find no evidence of anything unusual. The woman continued to appear to John, and he vomited straw, rushes, pins, nails, brambles and needles: each time his mouth was examined, each time there was no evidence of trickery. Later he saw a witch going through his window, carrying a mouse, but now saying he was going to get better. Straight away John began to recover. The people of Penzance were alarmed, because this could only be explained by witchcraft. The justices identified two particular suspects and on 27 July 1686 Jane Noel (also known as Nickless) and Betty Seeze were tried at Launceston but found not guilty of the crimes. No-one else was ever charged.

>> Turn left along the A30 for about 200 yards (185m) until you see the public footpath sign on your left. Cross over the road and follow the signs. You will now cross three fields, in each keeping to the hedges on your right, and then cross the stream which led you earlier to Carn Euny holy well.

As you cross the stile, you pass on your left Brane Barrow, a well-preserved Neolithic tomb 20 feet (6m) in diameter and 6½ feet (2m) high.

>> Where the path becomes a walled track continue to follow the footpath signs through Cardinney Farm until you arrive at the end of the drive. Continue straight on, crossing the track and then at the cross-roads going down the side of the house.

You are now walking part of the Tinners' Way, dating from the Bronze Age, roughly 2,000 BC and used to transport tin and copper from the mines around St Just to the port at St Michael's Mount, where it was traded with merchants for forwarding to Brittany and Mediterranean ports.

>> Go through the large iron gate to the junction of paths, and take the one on your left. Walk past the house on your right, and follow the path through the hamlet of Brane. Turn first left then immediately right and you arrive at your car.

PENZANCE

ARE THESE THE REAL PIRATES?

As you stand on the promenade, look out for a large group of men, wet and bedraggled, walking wearily up the shingle towards you. Who are they and why are they here?

In the early hours of a stormy night in 1760 an Algerian corsair, the *Cavallo Bianco*, foundered on Chimney Rocks just off Penzance. In no time at all the vessel began to break up and the crew jumped into the cold, dark, boiling waters. Fortunately they were close to shore and well over a hundred, though exhausted, reached safety and headed up Western Green beach. As always a group of locals had gathered to watch the drama unfold, but all thoughts of assistance dissipated as it became apparent that these were no ordinary sailors - they were dark skinned, carrying scimitars and wearing strange clothes. They were a pirate crew from North Africa. The watchers knew of their fearsome reputation. Only the previous century just such a pirate ship had crept into the harbour at night and carried off several men, women and children, who were never seen again. This had entered into the collective memory of Penzance. Was this a repeat visit? The Volunteers, armed and trained to defend the town against attack, were called out but the pirates were too tired and too disoriented to put up any resistance. They were rounded up, lodged in the 'Folly House' and for several weeks kept in quarantine before being taken to Falmouth.

Not all the pirate crew were so fortunate. Over the next day or so a total of fourteeen battered bodies were thrown up onto the sands. The town authorities acted swiftly: the bodies were buried where they were found, deep in the sand but without any religious ceremony, Christian or otherwise. That is how it was done in those days. But because of this the souls of these pirates remain earthbound at that spot until they receive a proper burial. Many people have seen them walking across the shingle on Western Green at low tide on dark, stormy nights, their scarred, distorted, wet faces pleading for assistance from the living to sever their earthly ties. As you pass the open-air swimming pool and walk onto the promenade, look down onto the beach towards Chimney Rocks. You may be able to help.

... THE BLACK DOG RETURNS ...

Many years ago a French ship moored here. A sailor was posted on watch, and when his crewmates returned he told them of a small black dog which had been a nuisance in trying to get aboard. None of his colleagues saw the dog, as it had gone. That same evening the sailor became unwell. His condition deteriorated and he died later that night.

Some time later a small fishing boat moored overnight at the South Pier in the harbour, and the crew decided to go to the Dolphin Tavern for a few drinks. One of them stayed behind to keep watch, and when his crewmates got back he told them of a friendly little black dog which had come aboard almost immediately they had left and had kept him company. It had stayed with him the whole evening but had run off just moments before the others returned.

Next day the men left to fish in Mount's Bay where they were caught in an unexpected storm. The crew struggled to keep control, and eventually the winds died down. But one of the crew was missing - the one who had seen the black dog. Was he a victim of the black dog of Penzance? We always take great care as we walk through the town. It just may be about still.

... AN UNSETTLED GHOST IS HERE.

In the early part of the nineteenth century, Quay Street was a fashionable area reflecting the town's wealth and trade. One house though became empty and neglected and two sailors broke in to spend the night there rather than return to their ship in the harbour. They hadn't been in long before they were woken by loud noises. They lay still, as heavy footsteps came up the stairs. Dressing quickly, they were mightily relieved to see in the dim light another sailor come in. He too must be looking for a room for the night. But this young sailor crossed the room and walked straight through the wall! Not surprisingly the two young men fled. They were convinced this was neither a dream nor an hallucination. This was a real man, of physical substance, dressed in sailor's uniform. Then it dawned on them: that uniform had been updated several decades ago. Now really frightened, they headed for the nearest inn to drown their fears, but the drinkers told them theirs was not an unusual occurrence: other people had seen the ghost and their descriptions were always the same.

Some years later, in 1813, the house had become uninhabitable and was pulled down. The workmen made a grim discovery. They found a skeleton walled up in a bedroom - the very same room in which the two sailors had seen the ghost. It appears that another young sailor had returned to Penzance after many years at sea, bringing all his accumulated wages. Unwisely, when he was drinking in the inn nearby he began to boast about this money. He was never seen again. At the time it was a reasonable assumption that he had returned to sea, but after the skeleton was found people put two and two together and decided that he had been robbed, murdered and bricked up in the wall. Because of this tragic end to his life, his spirit cannot find rest. To this very day it still troubles people living on the site.

LUDGVAN

THE CONSEQUENCE OF FORBIDDEN LOVE

On 9 November 1811 the parish clerk recorded the wedding at Ludgvan church of Henry Polgreen and Sarah Treman. On 12 August 1820 *The Royal Cornwall Gazette* reported the trial and conviction two days earlier of Sarah Polgreen for the murder of her husband. Between those two dates lay a tragedy. The marriage was not a success and it was marked by disillusion and bitterness. Then Sarah fell in love with a neighbour, Thomas Sampson, an itinerant horse dealer who went by the name of 'Yorkshire Jack'. As divorce was not possible in those days there was no way in which she could be free to live with him. Except one: she poisoned her husband. It wasn't long though before she was arrested, stood trial without legal representation, was convicted and sentenced "*to be hanged by the neck until dead*" two days later at Bodmin Gaol. Her body was not to be buried but used for medical dissection.

Most people felt sorry for the poor soul. They knew how badly Sarah had been treated by her cantankerous husband and how viciously his temper had been vented on her. There was little doubt she had been encouraged and possibly even helped in the dreadful deed by Yorkshire Jack. And they believed in the age-old folklore that no child baptised in Ludgvan's holy well could be hanged: this could only lead to disaster for the village.

On that terrible August morning, Sarah begged for Yorkshire Jack to be allowed to accompany her to the scaffold. Just before eight o'clock, as a crowd gathered to watch, the pair walked slowly hand in hand, embraced, kissed and whispered until the hangman made clear that the moment had come. Sarah looked directly and steadily into Yorkshire Jack's eyes: "*You will?*", she asked. "*I will*," he replied. She climbed the scaffold and he disappeared into the crowd. Moments later Sarah was dangling limply at the end of a rope.

Within days fear spread through Ludgvan. The white-shrouded figure of Sarah's ghost, its neck clearly displaying the marks of a rope burned into the white flesh, had been seen digging at the grave of her husband, Henry Polgreen. Others saw it walking slowly along the road and up the steps towards the grave yard's entrance.

Yorkshire Jack was never the same. He lost his outgoing persona, he became solitary and unkempt. For years he wandered the lanes, constantly looking over his shoulder. The ghost of Sarah Polgreen walked behind his every step, the tapping of her shoes clearly audible. Finally he left Lugdvan, and local gossips maintained that he had, in front of the scaffold, promised Sarah he would become her husband. To try to escape from his tormented self he went to sea. And inexorably the date came for him to fulfil his pledge to Sarah.

That night, his ship was heading towards Mount's Bay from the Mediterranean when a tremendous storm blew up. As the clock struck twelve Yorkshire Jack was met by Sarah Polgreen and the Devil. Other sailors heard the sounds of her footsteps on deck, following wherever he went. Then before anyone could stop him he lunged overboard. Amidst the crashing thunder and flashing lightning the sailors saw three figures riding a black cloud - Sarah Polgreen, the Devil and Yorkshire Jack. As soon as they had gone the storm died down and the ship went on its course to Penzance - and the unholy trio were never seen again.

MARAZION

HOW ST MICHAEL'S MOUNT WAS BUILT ...

As the great sweep of Mount's Bay unfolds you catch the first glimpse of a fairy-tale rising 240 feet out of the shimmering sapphire sea, separated from the mainland by a causeway which is itself covered at every high tide. This is St Michael's Mount. Now this magical island has a twelfth-century church, a medieval castle, an exotic garden and an ancient harbour. It was not always so, and we know how it came to be built.

In the days when giants lived in Cornwall they made their homes on the tops of hills - Carn Galver, Trencrom, Carn Brea, St Agnes Beacon all had resident giants. But one had no hill. Years ago, the area which we now call Mount's Bay was heavily wooded, so here, in this wood giant Cormoran decided to build a hill, higher than the surrounding trees to give a vantage point from which he could survey the countryside and be able to watch anyone, friend or foe, approaching from a considerable distance. He was very careful when it came to choosing the building materials, selecting suitably pale chunks of quartz from neighbouring moors in West Penwith. Although he was as tall as a mine stack, in common with other giants he was rather lazy, soon tired of the construction work and after eating several barrels of pilchards or a whole fat bullock would go to sleep, but as giants always do made sure his wife Cormelian did most of the heavy labour. To and fro she toiled on the long journey from the hills to the Mount, carrying the huge rocks in her apron and piling them one on top of the other. As it neared completion the Mount was given its Cornish name of *carreg luz enkuz*, 'the grey rock in the wood'. Poor Cormelian was not impressed. At the end of every day she was exhausted from lifting massive pieces of granite and carrying them through the forest. Her only thought was to see the job completed as quickly as possible. Then one day she noticed an outcrop of greenstone not too far from the grey rock. Surely, she reasoned, this would do as well - and it was lighter to carry. So she decided to cheat - as giants did. Waiting until her husband was asleep she broke off a great chunk, put it in her apron and hurried towards the Mount. This though awoke Cormoran. Straight away he noticed that his wife had substituted green rock for grey. Furious at her disobedience and deception he flew into a giant-sized rage and aimed a great kick which sent her head over heels. Her apron flew open and the greenstone fell into the water halfway between the hill they were building and the shore - where it has remained ever since. It is now called Chapel Rock, taking its name from the little chapel built on it centuries ago but demolished in 1645 when Parliamentary forces laid siege to the castle.

Though hurt, Cormelian recovered but not long afterwards (by our human time-scale) met her death accidentally. Her husband and the giant of Trecrobben, whom we have already met, used to spend a good deal of their time playing a game of throwing large boulders about. Indeed, many of those littering West Penwith are the consequences, while on the Mount itself you can still see the granite slabs and piles of rough cuboid rocks which were thrown from Trecrobben, an indication of how eagerly they pursued their sport. The two giants also shared a giant cobbler's hammer to repair their shoes which again they would throw to one another whenever it was needed. One day as it flew from Trencrom, Cormelian was so absorbed in her daily routines - no doubt organised by Cormoran - that she didn't see it in the air and by mistake it smashed into her skull, killing her outright. The roars of the two giants were like booming cracks of thunder and caused horrendous storms at sea. So disconsolate were they - even the previously uncaring Cormoran - that they lifted up the Mount and laid her to rest underneath. She is still here. If you look down the well you will see her eye looking back at you. Overcome with grief and remorse at killing his friend's wife, the Giant of Trecrobben died soon afterwards, leaving his treasure buried deep in the cairns there, where it remains in glittering piles guarded by platoons of fierce spriggans.

So what happened to Cormoran? Did he come to a sticky end? As a matter of fact, he did. Cormoran spent much of his time raiding the neighbourhood and carrying off sheep and cattle either on his back or slung from his belt. After putting up with this for some time, the folk offered a large reward to any-one who could get rid of this giant-sized terror. That included Jack the Giant Killer, a miner's son living near St Agnes. Jack evolved a plan. He dug a pit and covered it with sticks and straw then, standing on the far side facing the Mount, blew his horn. Down rushed Cormoran, falling straight into the trap. With one mighty blow of his pickaxe, Jack killed the giant and then filled the pit with earth. For this gallant achievement King Arthur himself presented Jack with a magnificent sword and a belt inscribed in gold

This is the valiant Cornishman
Who slew the giant Cormoran.

WALK DIRECTIONS

Distance 7 Miles (11.42km) Time 3½ hours
Map   OS Landranger 203 513310 Terrain Easy along the beach and Coast Path, with a gentle climb on your return journey before equally gentle descents on footpaths.
Car Parking. Leave your car in one of the car parks at Marazion.

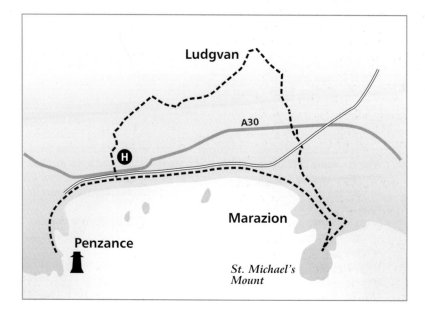

>> Walk down any of the passageways to the beach. A flight of stone steps takes you to Chapel Rock, dropped here by Cormelian as her husband Cormoran kicked her.

>> A broad cobbled causeway leads over to the Mount. This is open about three hours each side of high water, although will differ according to the onshore winds. It is quite safe as long as you make careful note of the time and the tides.

The first Archpriest of St Michael's, William Morton, was responsible for constructing the original stone causeway, assisted by the Bishop of Exeter who called upon sinners to make financial contributions as a way of easing their consciences. Interestingly, the Domesday Book of 1086 does not mention the island we now see but records an area about thirty times its present size. Old manuscripts tell us that at one time a forest covered this area and at exceptionally low water it is possible to see the remains of a petrified forest around the Mount, which has been taken to support the belief that it was the final remnant of Lyonesse.

>> Retrace your steps to the beach at Marazion and walk across the sand towards Penzance. Otherwise follow the signs for the Coast Path which runs along the top of the wall, but meanders quite a lot to cross several streams.

>> Continue until you reach the gardens which run alongside the main road, still keeping to the footpath signed to Penzance. This will take you into the town, walking alongside the A30, to search out the locations of the folklore.

>> Retrace your steps from Penzance until you reach and go across the A30. Follow the signs for Gulval, which means walking alongside the main road for a while and then taking the first road left, climbing gently as you go, away from the sea.

>> From the church walk along the lane which is diagonally right, signed 'Public Footpath'. This becomes a track, still ascending gently, and leads across two fields with woodland to your left, and into the hamlet of Tolver. Go through the houses and when you arrive at a junction with a surfaced road, turn right. This road bends first to the left and then on the right bend is a signed Public Footpath to your left. Go over the stile and across the field to Tregarthen.

>> Keep on the same path through the hamlet and follow the signs for Ludgvan. The path becomes a surfaced road, passing houses and roads on both your right and left, but keep walking, gently ascending again, until you reach the junction with B3309.

>> Go onto this road and as it turns sharply right you will see the church on your left. *This is where Henry Polgreen and Sarah Treman were married, where Henry was buried and where Sarah's ghost has been seen.*

>> Leave the church and turn left along the B3309. At the telephone box turn right onto the public footpath. Ignore the next footpath sign on your left and continue straight ahead until you cross a stile and emerge onto a surfaced road. From now on you are heading towards St Michael's Mount, which remains your focal point.

>> With the house opposite, turn right amd walk along this road to its junction with A30. Here turn right again and within a few yards take the signed Public Footpath on your left. Go over the stile and through the fields, keeping the Mount in front view and then woodland on your left.

In ancient times this was all unpassable marshland. Legend has it that here is where the last wolf in Cornwall lived until it was killed by local farmers after devouring a child.

When you reach A394 go under it and keep on the footpath, still with woodland to your left, until you walk through a short section before arriving at the railway line. The path takes you over the railway, where you turn right and walk alongside the stream to Marazion. Here you will join the Coast Path and your car.

GERMOE

ONE CASTLE, SO MANY DARK DEEDS ...

In a hollow running down to the broad sweep of Praa Sands just east of Hoe Point, you will find Pengersick Castle. Although it has adopted the title, is castellated with embattled turrets and has a machicolated gate, it never had any war-like role. Tales of some of its previous owners though will chill your blood - and make you smile.

The castle was built by the first Lord of Pengersick, a man with aspirations to social climbing who, with this in mind, planned to marry his son and heir to a much older lady connected to the Godolphins. This elderly - and plain - maiden was certainly eager to get her hands on both the young man and the castle, but all her attempts to encourage his affections were abortive. Eventually she got the message and sought help from the witch of Fraddam, but even love potions brewed specifically for her didn't work. Finally the old man decided that the only way to join the two families was to marry her himself - and she agreed.

One of the first things the new Lady of Pengersick did was to bring the witch's niece into her household, a poor but beautiful girl called Bitha. She though was not as innocent as one might think and had soon so ingratiated herself with her new mistress that she was appointed her personal maid, a post which gave her opportunity to see and speak to young Pengersick. Now Bitha had helped both her aunt and the Lady when they were weaving their spells, so we shouldn't be surprised that the inevitable happened and the young couple fell in love. But the situation was complicated. The stepmother was not at all pleased. Although she had married the older Pengersick she still had designs on the younger one and never let any opportunity pass to ensnare him. This, too, failed. Soon, as love does, it turned to uncontrollable jealousy. She again resorted to witchcraft but Bitha had by now acquired enough knowledge of the black arts from her aunt to counteract these spells.

The Lady next decided to get her revenge - and revenge would be sweet - using her husband. She persuaded the old man that his son really was passionately in love with her and that to avoid any unpleasantness she had to hide herself away in the tower - indeed, she feared for her honour, and on one occasion had to threaten him with a knife until he left. The best way out was for the father to hire a gang of sailors to kidnap his son, take him to some foreign land and sell him as a slave. Oh and by the way, there is some urgency as we are soon to have an heir of our own! Besotted and enraged, the old man agreed. Now she had only to get rid of the old lord! She discussed with Bitha a plan to poison him at supper.

Fortunately, the young Pengersick avoided all this scheming. He saw no future here, so left. For a long time no one heard of him. At the castle though the plotting and counter-plotting continued, with both the mistress and maid determined to get their hands on old Pengersick's wealth, until he died from the effects of poison administered by his 'loving' wife.

Many years later, the young man, now himself Lord of Pengersick, returned. He had not wasted his time. Firstly, while in the Far East, he had married a princess and brought her home with him. Secondly, he had made himself expert in all the magical sciences of the lands he had visited. He was a talented sorcerer himself. But he didn't need to use any of those skills when he arrived to confront his stepmother. She had shut herself in the tower, her skin covered with scales like a serpent, the after-effects of all the poisons she had been distilling. Rather than see him she threw herself into the sea. Bitha fared little better. Now living on the Downs in St Hilary, she too had suffered from the poisonous fumes she had inhaled and from her dealings with evil. Her beauty disappeared and her skin became the colour of a toad - though some say it was the old Lady who had turned her into one. One night she was working at her witchcraft, the flames from her fire rising high above her roof, when local folk nailed up her door and put turf over the chimney until she was suffocated by the vapours that came from the pot in which she was brewing her infernal charms.

Almost immediately the stepmother's ghost began to haunt her apartment, wandering about the place until, by his magic powers, Pengersick had it transmuted into a large adder and confined to a hole in the Hoe, the headland west of Pengersick Cove. Local folk still report seeing it. However, over the next few years Pengersick became so interested in sorcery that he spent nearly all his time practising. Fires blazed in the tower day and night, and flames reached into the sky above the battlements when he changed base metals into silver and gold. If the fire went out he relit it with sparks drawn from the sun through a magic crystal. It didn't take long for him to become known as a powerful magician and, not surprisingly, no-one tried to take advantage of the fact that he left the management of his estate to his staff. Until one person from the Mount carried off one of his fattened sheep, its feet tied together and strung over his neck. Just at that moment Pengersick was looking into his crystal, saw what was happening and cast a spell which transfixed the thief to the spot all night with the tide rising around him and the sheep hanging from his neck. Next morning Pengersick released the thief and gave him the sheep with the warning that if he interfered with his flocks again his reaction would be considerably worse.

More years went by. One of the Pengersicks' numerous descendants, the beautiful Lamorna, married a Welsh prince who had come to Pengersick Castle for instruction in magic. When he got back home the prince sent a load of black stones to Pengersick from which the magician extracted a sort of liquid fire. He made a mistake though and the fire burst its pans. He and all his books and treasures were burned. Nothing was left of the castle but bare walls.
Now most of the Pengersicks were a war-like crowd, and instead of looking after their farms or developing tin mines like other landed gentry, spent their time abroad wherever fighting was going on. When the youngest son of the last Lord of Pengersick was about twenty years of age and travelling far to the east he met a beautiful Princess. Regretably from his point of view she was already betrothed, but he still found opportunity to seduce her - and as lovers do swore he would return and marry her.

Within a short while of arriving home he had married a local lady, but after a year or so no son and heir had appeared. News came of renewed fighting in the East so off he went again only to find that the former princess was now the reigning Queen. Once more he declared undying love. This time however he was defeated in battle and immediately left for home, abandoning the Queen to her fate. She managed to escape, and knowing that Pengersick's castle was near a place where her people often went for tin, she too set sail for Cornwall.

However, when the treacherous lover returned home he found his wife with a newly-born baby. He was angry she had not told him about her pregnancy before he had left but nonetheless settled comfortably into his castle - until one night the foreign Queen arrived at the gate. In her arms she too held a baby but, despite her pleading, he refused to let her in. To prevent this argument being overheard he took the Queen down to the sea - then threw her and her son over the cliff. Pengersick however had forgotten one critical fact: the Queen was herself a powerful sorceress. As she died her soul slipped from her body and into that of a pure white hare.

The following day Pengersick went hunting and as he galloped at full speed along the cliffs a white hare, its eyes like coals of fire, ran under his horse's hoofs causing it to stumble and roll into the sea. Neither it nor its rider were ever seen again.

The next family to own Pengersick Castle were the Millitons, and they fared no better. Apparently, some time during the reign of Henry VIII, one of them killed a man in a drunken brawl in London. Before he could be brought to trial, this Milliton fled to sea where somehow or other he became so rich that *"when he loaded his ass with gold, the weight was so great as to break the poor animal's back."* Only years later did he return to this country, bought the manor of Pengersick and strengthened the castle - to defend himself from any officers of the law who might try to apprehend him for his crime.

Like the Pengersicks, few of the Millitons could be said to have lived in marital bliss. One, William, just did not get on with his wife, Honor. Their relationship became so strained that William suggested they should try to begin anew, and mark their good intentions by dining together, something they hadn't done for a long time. Honor agreed. Their servants prepared a special meal, the pair were as pleasant as possible towards each other, and at the end William proposed a toast to their future. Again, Honor agreed. He drained his glass; she did the same. But that was not the end of their romantic evening of reconciliation. Honor laughed out loud as she announced that she had poisoned his drink and he had just three minutes to live. Nonplussed, he replied that he too had poisoned her drink and she had only five minutes to live. Honor was satisfied with this: she had, she said, two minutes in which to experience her triumph, and to express her feelings about him with her foot!

WALK DIRECTIONS

Distance 5½ miles (8.85km) Time 3½ hours
Map OS Landranger 203 540295 Terrain The outward leg of the walk follows every nuance of this tortuous coastline, up and down. There are some modest slopes from sea level to 240 feet (74m). The return part uses field paths and ancient tracks.
Car Parking Park just above the beach at Perranuthnoe, opposite the Post Office.

>> From the car park turn left towards the beach, and left again onto a surfaced lane. When you reach the fork bear, walking gently uphill, and at 'Blue Burrow' cottage bear right again to follow the yellow arrow waymark along an unmade track towards the sea, following it round to the left.

>> At the next waymark post go down right on the track through the field and turn sharp left through the gap, now following the edge of the field to the Coast Path.

>> This can be seen clearly as it runs along the top of the cliffs and beaches, facing the sea, and will take you all the way to Praa Sands.
Perranuthnoe is where, legend has it, the sole survivor of the Lost Land of Lyonesse, a Trevellian, set foot on shore after escaping the flood.

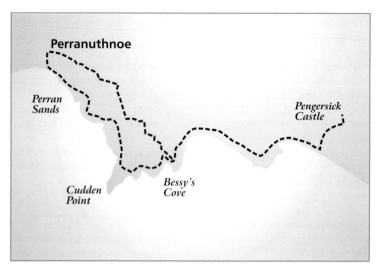

On the map: Perranuthnoe, Perran Sands, Pengersick Castle, Cudden Point, Bessy's Cove

>> The magnificent spur of rocks stretching out in front is Cudden Point. On your way there you will walk via a number of stiles and fields along the edge of Trebarvah Cliff, Trevean Cove, and Stackhouse Cliffs and Cove, above which is Acton Castle. *In the nineteenth, century workmen found a skull in the cliff at Trevean Cove and were haunted by its ghost until they replaced it.*
From Cudden Point the view to your right opens up across Mount's Bay, with St Michael's Mount holding centre stage. In front of you is the Lizard.
On a calm day, if you look into the sea from Cudden Point you will see a silver table floating below the surface. One of the less salubrious Lords of Pengersick was holding a sailing party off here one fine day and had provided a silver table spread with rich food and fine wines for his guests. The water was calm and they were ill-prepared when towards evening without warning the boat overturned and sank, drowning all its passengers. Old fishermen will tell you that if you listen carefully and the weather is right, not only will you see the table but hear the guests' chattering and laughter below the waves.
>> From Cudden Point, follow the Coast Path steeply uphill and then across the inner slope of the headland above both Piskies and Bessy's Cove. At the latter, go through a gate and pass an old stone fisherman's cottage before bearing left towards the houses. Keep to the path round the edge of Prussia Cove.
Smuggling clings romantically to this coastline and it is not difficult to imagine 'freetraders' stealing through the mist with cargoes of tea, tobacco, spirits, silks and china. Such nostalgia hides the casual brutality which was part of the trade. In the eighteenth century this series of coves and inlets was the preserve of the Carter family, and particularly of John and his brother Henry who ran a smuggling enterprise with flair and efficiency. It was John's fascination and identification with Frederick the Great, Emperor of Prussia, which led to his nickname of 'The King of Prussia'. The name stuck and the original Porth Leah became 'The King of Prussia's Cove', which has since been shortened further. You will recognise it from the big caves under the cliff, and the remains of the King of

Prussia's jetty cut in the rock. The ridges on the rocks are the tracks made by the Carter brothers for their wagons. On the top left in the cleft of trees is the entrance to one of the tunnels which went directly up to John's house which stands at the top of the cliff. John and Henry even fortified the cove with small canons on each headland, to discourage Excise men from coming close inshore.

>> Continue on the Coast Path around Kenneggy Cliff where one path plunges down to the beach but you descend more gently to the left to Hoe Point. and the broad sweep of Praa Sands. Pengersick Castle is through the second gate on your left. *All that is left of the castle which had such a sinister reputation is one of the towers, incorporated into another building. It all looks very peaceful now - but not then ... There are tales that the treasure of a Portuguese ship, the 'San Antonio', which was wrecked at nearby Gunwalloe in 1526, was brought to Pengersick Castle and hidden in its walls. Some people claim the treasure is still here and that the ghosts of the crew and the men who plundered the cargo still haunt the castle looking for their booty.*

>> Retrace your steps to Bessy's Cove and continue along the Coast Path. Go past the entrance of the curious granite-built 'Porth-enalls', and follow its drive. At the second gate head towards the picturesque cove-side cottages.

>> When you arrive in front of a thatched cottage turn right up an unmade track. At the large wooden gate with tall granite gate-posts turn left, keeping to the track which is now leading away from the coast. You will now climb gradually until you reach a line of granite posts which divide the track in two. Keep to the left-hand side and at the metalled road turn right. This road is very winding but in about half a mile, after the second bend, reaches a hamlet with farm buildings on your right. Go over the stile opposite on your left just past the field gate.

>> Follow the public footpath sign over a stile in a wall and across the field. In the left hand corner is another stile, after which you should keep to the right-hand boundary of the next field, and walk behind Acton Castle. At the garage turn right, through a wooden gate and cross the lane where you see the sign 'Trevean Farm'.

>> In front of the bungalow at Trevean Farm, turn left along a rough track and, where this bends left towards the cluster of farm buildings, go onto a stony track for just a few paces before you come to a Public Footpath sign. Follow this, ascending to your right Go up the steps, turn right into a field, still following the 'Public Footpath' signs, then turn left along the edge of the field to the stone stile at the top. In the next field, cross diagonally right and then keep to the right.

>> You are now heading towards Trebarvah Farm, where you cross the farm lane and a stile. Turn left in the farmyard and take the signed footpath over a stile into the corner of a field. Keep the hedge on your right and cross the stile in the next corner. Go through another field, still with the hedge on your right, and walk along the path between two hedges. Go over the stile and across two fields, keeping to their right-hand boundaries, before joining a narrow track which takes you over a stile. Keep parallel to the telegraph poles as you cross the field and then through the kissing gate, where you emerge onto the road opposite Ye Olde Victoria Inn.

>> Turn left and follow the road through the village to your car.

HELSTON AND LOE POOL

WHAT'S IN A NAME?

The area was once the resort of fiery dragons and even of the Devil himself. We have already read about the latter's habit of throwing stones around, but surely the most impressive impact occurred here. This time the Devil was flying over Cornwall intent on malevolence but was interrupted by St Michael. A fight ensued, and finding himself outwitted the Devil tore the lid off the entrance to Hell and threw the huge granite block at the saint. Fortunately his aim was inaccurate, the rock missed and Hell's Stone fell to the ground - right on the spot where Helston now stands. So Helston got its name - literally. To be precise, the large granite block landed in the courtyard of an inn - the Angel, no less - and was built into its west wall.

At the time this aerial combat between Satan and St Michael was going on, a little old lady was picking wild flowers on the shores of Loe Bar. She saw the titanic struggle, heard the terrible crash as the Stone flew from the Devil's hands, and was terrified to see a dragon flying above her, heading for the town after being summoned by the Devil to come to his assistance. Was she relieved when the creature missed its mark and fell into the lake! She made sure it had drowned and then ran into Helston, shouting the news and waving her flowers - the first-ever Flora Dance.

Towards Loe Pool from Porthleven

To be fair, the conventional view is that the town's name derives from *helles*, meaning 'old court', and *ton*, denoting its Saxon manorial origin. Dare one speculate though that the name recalls a cult which worshipped the sun and that the Furry or Flora Dance when the past takes over on 8 May each year, was a pagan welcome to Spring but which over the years has been transformed to commemorate St Michael, the town's patron?

Loe Bar figures in another, very different story. One summer's evening a young man from Cury, Lutey by name, was walking on Berepper Sands and came across a beautiful mermaid left high and dry by the outgoing tide. Being the sort of fellow he was, he carried her gently to the edge of the waves and let her go. Here,

Morvena, as the mermaid was called, gave him a golden comb and promised her help should he ever find himself in difficulty: to summon her he only had to comb his hair three times and call her name. He was also granted three wishes: he chose protection from witchcraft, an ability to control spirits and to keep these powers in his family for ever.

As all mermaids do, Morvena tried to lure Lutey into the depths of the sea but he was having none of that, so she gave him nine years of freedom before she would return to claim him for herself. From that day Lutey prospered. He became a famous white wizard with the power to heal the sick and help the poor, and over time forgot about the probationary period - until exactly nine years later. He was fishing on Loe Pool when Morvena returned. Hearing her calling him, Lutey leapt overboard to join her. He was never seen again and his fishing companion had the difficult task of breaking the news to his family. Interestingly, several of Lutey's descendants became white wizards and witches while others inherited his healing powers. The mermaid had kept her promise.

Then there is a strange tale about Whealor Mine, nearby. When he was charging a hole with blasting powder, a young tinner made an error in his calculations and he and an older colleague had the unenviable task of removing the powder to start the process again. Tragically it exploded and the men were blown to pieces. When their remains were brought to the surface they were in such a terrible state that one of the miners picked them up on a shovel and threw them into the engine furnace, to save the feelings of the men's families. From that day the engine-house was haunted by a pack of small, black dogs which were seen by many of the boiler-men and stokers, and though few tinners would speak of the apparitions none liked to be in this part of the mine - and certainly never alone!

WALK DIRECTIONS

Distance 5 miles (8km)   Time   3 hours
Map   OS Landranger 203 639259 Terrain   Undemanding level paths and surfaced
                                                     tracks, varying from a densely wooded
                                                     river valley to open sandy coast.
Car parking   Park at the Penrose Amenity Area car park, off B3304

>> At the far end of the car park go through a gap to the left of the Amenity Park sign and turn right along the concrete drive, passing the sign to 'Lower Nansloe'.

>> In about half a mile (800m) you will pass the former chimney stack of Castle Wary mine, which in the eighteenth century produced lead and silver. After a further 50 yards (46m) turn right through the gate and emerge onto the causeway over Loe Marsh, keeping to the right. Cross this causeway and go through the gate, then turn left along a broad track through the woods of Oak Grove. At the end of the woodland cross a stile before turning left onto a lane just before the farm buildings.

>> Go past the bird hide on your left and through the gate in front of Helston Lodge on your right, continuing up the drive to where it forks. Take the right fork towards Penrose House.
   There is a good view of Penrose House from here. From Norman times, the estate has been the ancestral home of only two families, first the Penrose family from the late twelfth century, and then the Rogers family from the eighteenth century until they gave it to the National Trust in 1974.

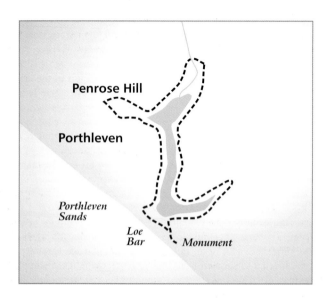

Penrose Hill

Porthleven

Porthleven
Sands

Loe
Bar

Monument

>> Follow the drive across the parkland and bear left in front of the former stable
block. Continue alongside the Loe on the old carriageway, which leads you
through Bar Walk Plantation as far as Bar Lodge on the lakeside path around the
head of a reed-choked inlet.

*The Loe, from the Cornish 'logh', is the largest natural freshwater lake in
Cornwall. Originally it was the estuary of the River Cober but as the build-up of
silt washed down-river from more than thirty tin and copper mines operating in
the river's catchment area added to the encroaching shingle spits at the seaward
end, the formidable 'bar', now a wide expanse of sand and shingle, was created.
The shingle may have come from an offshore deposit of flint on the seabed which
has been formed into a spit by both onshore and longshore drift. The river had
been navigable until sometime just before the thirteenth century the 'bar'
separated the pool from the sea and dammed the river, and Helston had been a
thriving port. Though it now provides a convenient short-cut across the mouth of
the Cober, linking the fishing port of Porthleven with Gunwalloe, it was not
welcomed by the merchants of Helston. Not only did they lose their tidal access to
the sea but they also had to contend with periodic flooding of the town mills when
the level of the lake rose through heavy rainfall. There is now an underground
culvert but for centuries the bar had to be broken open manually to release the
water.*

*Many people consider that when writing his 'Morte D'Arthur' Tennyson was
describing Porthleven Sands as the place where Arthur fought Mordred and that
Excalibur was thrown into Loe Pool, across which the dying King Arthur was
taken to Avalon by the sorrowing Queens. Take Tennyson's poems with you on the
walk and see what you think.*

>> Go through the gate and turn right, signed 'Loe Bar', on the Coast Path across
Porthleven beach, an area notorious for claiming many an unfortunate ship.

Ironically their destruction frequently became an important part of the local economy. Attempts by Customs officers to regulate the pillage of wrecked ships met with little success as they were outnumbered by crowds of plunderers and often intimidated. In 1748 Customs officials in Porthleven watched as villagers 'redistributed' 170 tons of Bordeaux wine from the 'Jonge Alacada' which was wrecked en route to Amsterdam. Then in 1817 a brig was beached here. Immediately a huge crowd fell on it armed with pick-axes, hatchets and crowbars, plus utensils to carry off its cargo of wine. Fighting broke out and in the drunken melee a young boy was drowned and on their way home two men fell by the wayside and perished from alcoholism and hypothermia.

\>\> Head towards the white cross on the opposite headland.

This simple stone commemorates the loss of the 44-gun frigate HMS Anson here in December 1807, whilst on its way to blockade Brest. Despite the ship being beached on Loe Bar the locals couldn't save over a hundred people from being drowned. The victims were buried, as was the custom, in unmarked graves on the open cliff, because it couldn't be determined that they were baptised Christians. One of those watching, Henry Trengrouse, was so frustrated that he devoted the rest of his life to developing a rocket apparatus for firing a line onto ships from shore. After many attempts, in 1816 he succeeded in perfecting his invention and it became standard life-saving equipment for Coastguards. The Government awarded him £50, the Royal Society gave him 30 guineas and the Tzar of russia sent him a diamond ring and a silver medal. Trengrouse died penniless in 1854, but Parliament changed the law to provide Christian burial to those drowned in shipwrecks.

\>\> Retrace your steps to the sandy path and cross the bridge that leads alongside Carminowe Creek. Walk along the boardwalk around its head to join the track which leads you past Lower Pentire house. Just before the surface becomes metalled, turn left. Go through a gate, keeping to the edge of the field, and when you arrive at a bench continue to follow the field edge but now walking away from the water. Pass through the gate onto a track through Degibna Wood.

\>\> As you leave the Wood turn right and go down the concrete lane. Pass through the kissing gate, signed to 'Degibna and Loe Pool' and up to the farm buildings. At the house take the left fork and go through the kissing gate. Follow this lane and keep walking anti-clockwise around the lake, crossing the wooden footbridge over the River Cober, the source of Loe Pool, where the lake succumbs to marshland and scrubby trees, but which are really the choked river.

\>\> Continue on this path which will take you back to your car.

BIBLIOGRAPHY

Acton, Bob (1989) *A View From St Agnes Beacon* Devoran: Landfall Publications

Addicoat, Ian, and Buswell, Geoff (2003) *Mysteries of the Cornish Coast*
Tiverton: Halsgrove

Bottrell, William (1880) *Traditions and Hearthside Stories of West Cornwall* Llanerch
Press

Caine, Margaret, and Gorton, Alan (2001) *Curiosities of Cornwall*
Seaforth: SB Publications

Courtney, M A (1973) *Cornish Feasts and Folklore* Wakefield: EP Publications

Garnett, William (1989) *Horrors and Hauntings in Cornwall* Padstow: Tabb House

Hunt, Robert (1865) *PopularRomances of the West of England*

Hunt, Robert (1881) *Romances and Superstitions of the West of England*

Hunt, Robert (1993) *Ghosts, Demons and Spectres in Cornish Folklore* Redruth: Tor Mark

James, Beryl (1988) *Tales of the Tinners' Way* Redruth: Dyllansow Truran

Jenner, Michael (1993) *Travellers' Companion to the West Country* London: Joseph

Jones, Sally (1980) *Legends of Cornwall* St Teath: Bossiney Books

Lacey, Robert (2003) *Great Tales from English History* London: Little, Brown

Stanier, Peter (1988) *The Work Of Giants* St Ives: St Ives Printing and Publishing Co.

Tangye, Michael (1988) *Carn Brea* Truro: Dyllansow Truran

Thomas, Charles (1985) *Exploration of a Drowned Landscape* London: Batsford

Tregarthen, Enys (1940) *Piskey Folk* New York: John Day

Tor Mark Press (1997) *Strange Tales of the Cornish Coast*

Turner, J (1973) *Ghosts of the South West* Newton Abbot: David and Charles

Weatherill, Craig, and Devereux, Paul (2001) *Myths and Legends of Cornwall*
'Wilmslow: Sigma'

White, Paul (1994) *Classic Cornish Anecdotes* Redruth: Tor Mark Press

Williams, Michael, and Chard, Paul (1978) *Penzance To Land's End*
St Teath: Bossiney Books

Wood, Michael (1999) *In Search of England* London: Viking

Front cover: Giant Bolster and helpers, St Agnes annual carnival
Back cover: Madgy Figgy's chair ladder, Tol-Pedn
Title page: Lanyon Quoit,, Bosullow Common